★ ★ ★ ★ ★ ★ ★ ★ ★ ★ ★ ★ ★ ★

YOURS FOR A MEETING
IN THE AIR

YOURS FOR A MEETING
IN THE AIR

60 YEARS WITH GOD AS MY CO-PILOT

CAPT. DON H. BELDIN

TATE PUBLISHING & *Enterprises*

Tate Publishing
& Enterprises

Tate Publishing is committed to excellence in the publishing industry. Our staff of highly trained professionals, including editors, graphic designers, and marketing personnel, work together to produce the very finest books available. The company reflects the philosophy established by the founders, based on Psalms 68:11,

"The Lord Gave The Word And Great Was The Company Of Those Who Published It."

If you would like further information, please contact us:

1.888.361.9473 | www.tatepublishing.com

Tate Publishing & Enterprises, llc | 127 E. Trade Center Terrace Mustang, Oklahoma 73064 USA

Published in the United States of America

ISBN: 978-1-6024700-2-6

07.01.08

This book is dedicated in loving memory to my dear parents, Rev. Howard E. and Violette D. Beldin, who prayed me through the flight experiences recounted in the chapters of this book. They now reside in their heavenly home enjoying their rewards for over forty years of faithful service in the Lord's service.

TABLE OF CONTENTS

Introduction   9

Big Trouble at 8,000 Feet   11

That Unforgettable Ride   15

Those Exciting First Lessons   19

Hayfield Flying   23

First Solo   27

A Summer Adventure   31

Reliving Those Barn Storming Days   37

How Much Was That Airplane?   41

The Thrill of Open Cockpit Flying   45

Hey! Wait for Me   51

Twenty Exciting Minutes in the Vultee BT-13   57

Who Turned out the Lights?   61

Something in the Air Besides Flying   65

Barn Yard Landing   69

'Round and 'Round We Go   73

Flying the Bamboo Bomber   77

Banner Towing   83

Emergency Crash Landing   87

Baby in a Shoe Box   91

Men That Impacted My Life   95

Getting Flight Experience the Hard Way   99

The Desires of Your Heart   105

The Rest of the Story   109

That Final Flight   113

Photo Gallery   115

INTRODUCTION

I'm not quite certain when I first met Don Beldin. It was around 8 or 9 years of age. What I do remember is watching his every move. You see, he was a pilot, and even at that young age, that's what I wanted to be as well. So, I would emmulate him. I would watch him during conversations with others. Listen to his prayers. Try to walk like he walked. Even copy his favorite colors as my own (red and black). I told my mother I just HAD to have a red and black banlon knit shirt, with a matching stretch belt. Over the years since, and as a result of my close observations, I have discovered him not only to be one of the finest pilots with whom I've flown, but also one of the most consistent Christians I have ever met. He has never wavered in his testimony or his commitment to his Lord. He will not know, at least on this earth, the impact he has had on my life.

Don took me flying for my first airplane ride when I was 10. How well I remember that flight in his Twin Navion. Every detail of that Monday afternoon is etched in my mind as if it were today. He helped launch my flying career, and was my mentor in those early days. I would say he still is. For over 40 years, he and his family have been close friends.

In 1964, he started what is now MISSIONARY FLIGHTS INTERNATIONAL, with that same Twin Navion. Don now sits as Chairman of the Board of this organization that operates a fleet of DC-3's to several island nations in the Carribean, including Haiti and the Dominican Republic. I don't believe it too far-fetched to say if it weren't for MFI, close to 1,000 missionaries would not receive their weekly supplies.

Don had the fortune to grow up in a time when aviation was still so new that it intrigued the entire nation. When he writes of "flying from one hayfield to another" and "buzzing the town's constable," I can only dream of such a time. On many days and nights I have found myself flying over those same fields in northern Illinois, and wondering what his early life as a pilot must have been like. Now, through this work, we all will know. He has the ability to captivate the reader.

Fortunately, Don never gets too technical for the non-flying reader. And yet, these true stories of his aerial escapades will captivate even the most seasoned aviator. (Buy a Stearman for $250.00?!) Don Beldin is a "pilots' pilot" in every sense of the word. He is truly a man of passion when it comes to his flying, and I am thrilled and honored that he has asked me to introduce this wonderful book to you. Now Don, when can we expect a sequel?

~Capt. Rick L. Ferrin
Boeing 757/767
UPS Airlines

BIG TROUBLE AT 8,000 FEET

The sun shown brightly through the cockpit windshield as we began our descent into Palm Beach International Airport. It was one of those VFR (which is pilot lingo for Visual Flight Rules) blue sky-fleecy white cloud days that was made for flying. On board were a pastor and five of his laymen. We had just finished an eight VIP Flight, visiting missionaries and holding services down island in the West Indies. VIP was an acronym for *"Vision, Inspiration, & Participation,"* providing mission-minded pastors and lay-people the opportunity to visit a near mission field and see first hand what missions is all about. It was a part of our *missionary flights* ministry of air support to missions.

The serenity of that moment was rudely interrupted by a sudden loud metallic sound coming from the right side of the aircraft. I was flying a twin engine, eight passenger Beech 18, and my immediate thought was that something catastrophic was happening to the right engine. I began shutting down the engine. Simultaneous to the metallic sound, my control yoke began to shake as if some giant was rapidly moving the tail elevator up and down. I felt my gut tightening in the pit of my stomach—we were in trouble, maybe BIG trouble! But what could it be? If the shaking of the control wheel was caused by the tail elevator coming loose, the aircraft could become uncontrollable. Wow! That metallic sound was deafening! With the constant shaking of the control wheel, how would this affect our landing at PBIA? I breathed a prayer of "help Lord" as I thought about what might be ahead in the next twenty minutes. Our routine flight had suddenly become anything but routine!

The airspeed indicator was hovering at 180 mph in our decent. The pastor who occupied the copilot seat looked outside his window and saw that the battery cover on top of the wing just inboard of the right engine had come loose and was flapping in the slipstream. That accounted for the deafening metallic sound. It wasn't the engine, so I came up with the power. I thought if I slowed the airplane down, maybe the fluttering would stop. I pulled the nose up and bled off the airspeed. As the airspeed came down to about 120, the nose started to pitch over. When pulling back on the control wheel didn't bring the nose up—*I knew I was losing control of the aircraft!*

But I'm getting ahead of my story.

I think I was born to fly. From my earliest recollection I loved airplanes. My prized toy as a five-year-old boy was a metal airplane. As I got older, I whiled away the winter nights in Northern Illinois bent over the dining room table building model airplanes. This activity taught me a lot about how airplanes are made, how they fly, and what controls their flight.

Model airplanes were fun, but eventually it wasn't enough. I had to experience the real thing. *I needed to get a ride in a real airplane!* It was 1940, and at age twelve, unbeknownst to my parents, I bought a 1927 Model T Ford Roadster. Through this escapade I met a farmer who helped me get the old car running. Amazingly, I learned that he had a Piper Cub sitting in the corner of his hayfield, which he flew. Isn't is amazing how God puts the right people in the right place at the right time? His timing is always perfect! With that knowledge, I became his shadow. Every time I saw him I would beg him for a ride. It took two years, but finally, when he could stand it no longer, he gave in and said I'd get my ride the next Saturday. It seemed it would never come.

THAT UNFORGETTABLE RIDE

Instead of giving me a ride in his Cub as I expected, he arranged for a furloughing Navy pilot to give me a ride at old Hillcrest Airport outside Freeport, Illinois. Later I discovered why. On that Saturday, my farmer friend picked me up, and we drove the twenty-six miles to the airport. It was called Hillcrest Airport because the two grass runways intersected on the crest of a small hill. Takeoffs were started going up hill and then enough airspeed was gained for takeoff going down the other side. It was a barnstorming kind of airport with a rickety wooden hangar and a small office built into the back corner complete with a pot-bellied stove and old car seats to sit on.

There was an Aronca Chief sitting in front of the hangar. Yep, this was the plane in which I would experience the thrill of flying. Little did I know what a thrill this would be! My friend introduced me to the Navy pilot, and we climbed in. It was a two-place, side-by-side airplane, and we buckled in, or rather, he buckled in. There was only one long seat belt that covered both pilot and passenger. Since the pilot was bigger than I was, my part of the seat belt lay loosely across my lap. Outside stood my friend grinning from ear to ear. Did he know something I didn't know? Someone stepped to the front of the airplane and yelled, "Switch Off" and began turning the prop. From my model airplane days, I knew that turning the prop wound up the rubber band that would provide the power for flight. No, I didn't think there was a rubber band that he was winding up! After a few turns of the prop, he called out "Contact," and the pilot turned the ignition switch to "on" and responded "Contact." A quick flip of the prop and the engine came to life. Wow! I couldn't believe it! I was really going to fly!

We taxied out to the runway, he did a run-up to check the engine, and turned onto the grass runway, and we started the takeoff. As we became airborne, I looked out my side window and there was my friend standing in front of the hangar waving. I couldn't tell, but I'm sure he must have still had that grin on his face. As we climbed away from the airport, I was all eyes and ears. What an experience! I could see for miles, and the cars that were on the road looked like toys. As we climbed for altitude everything got smaller. It seemed like we were sitting on top of the world.

We leveled off at about 2,000 feet, and the pilot asked, "How you doing?"

"Good." I replied.

Then he said, "Would you like to do a loop?"

I knew what a loop was so I gamely said, "Sure."

I watched as he shoved the throttle all the way in, pushed forward on the stick, and after gaining some airspeed pulled it all the way back. Wow! I felt a force that I had never felt before. It nailed me to my seat and seemed to pull down on my face. The ground disappeared, and sky filled the windshield. Over the top of the loop the ground showed up again as we headed straight down. Again, the force of gravity socked me in my seat and pulled on my eyeballs as we rounded out the loop to level flight. I hardly knew what to say, but I managed to mutter something in response to his inquiry of how I liked that. Why was that twinkle in his eyes?

This was supposed to be a short hop to circle over my hometown, Warren, Illinois. So far it had been an aerobatic flight, but the worst was yet to come. He wasn't through yet! To this day I'm not sure what maneuver came next, but the left wing went down and the nose came up, and at the top of what probably was a chandel, I came out of my seat. That loose belt allowed a gap between my seat and the airplane seat. Hanging by the belt my head hit a cross bar in the top of the cabin. Instinctively I tried to raise my right arm up to push myself back into the seat. I then tried to raise my left arm but I couldn't move it either. Centrifugal force was at work. When the airplane returned to level flight I found myself back in my seat, and the world was right side up again.

My hometown looked very small from 1,000 feet, but I was able to pick out the Baptist church my dad pastored and the parsonage behind it where we lived. I spotted the town water tower that stood 100 feet high. I saw my high school,and the downtown stores where we shopped. The flight back to the airport was routine, no surprises, although I was hoping for some. As the airport came into view, I knew my first flight would soon be over, and I didn't want it to end. It had been all I imagined it would be, and then some. The little Aeronca Chief touched down lightly and rolled to a stop on the crest of the runway. I wasn't expecting the welcome I got when we taxied back and shut down in front of the hangar.

Before I could get out of the airplane, my friend rushed up to my open door with a bucket of water and a mop. I didn't get it until he said, "It's up to you to clean it up." Then I got it. He thought I had gotten sick and had tossed my lunch during the flight. But I hadn't. And now I knew why he had that grin on his face before the flight. He knew something I didn't know alright. He had told the Navy pilot to wring me out good in the hope that it would get this pesky kid off his back. It didn't work. The few aerobatics that the Aeronca

Chief was capable of doing just whet my appetite for more. I started taking lessons at Hillcrest Airport the next week.

★ ★ ★

THOSE EXCITING
FIRST LESSONS

I was almost fifteen and had two jobs that earned me a little money. Flying lessons at Hillcrest Airport were $6 an hour, including instructor. Still, when you were only making fifty cents an hour, six dollars seemed like a lot of money. Incidentally, that's how I was able to buy that 1927 Model T Roadster—but that's another story. So, that next week I rode to the airport with my friend with my $6 burning a hole in my pocket. Wow! I was really going to learn to fly!

The instructor was a short guy named Barney. Didn't look at all like a pilot. We rolled the yellow J-3 Cub out of the hangar, gassed it up, and climbed in. In a Piper Cub the instructor occupies the front seat and the student the rear seat. It always seemed to me to be an odd arrangement because the person sitting in the front seat completely blocks your view of the instrument panel. You had to peak around the side of the person, and if he was really big you couldn't catch more than an occasional glimpse of the instruments. There wasn't much up there on the panel—just airspeed, altimeter, tach, compass, engine oil pressure and temp gages, and that was about it. If you flew the Cub alone, you had to fly it from the back seat because of the weight of the engine and your weight. If you flew it from the front seat the center of gravity would be out of limits because of too much weight forward.

Fortunately, Barney was a small guy, so he didn't completely obliterate the panel. So off we went into the wild blue yonder to do some ninety degree turns.

Every time I would bank the airplane into a turn, the nose would drop below the horizon. I was losing altitude with every turn, and it wasn't long before Barney grabbed the front control stick abruptly, pulled the nose up into a steep climbing turn, then leveled off and rapped my knees good with a fast side to side motion with the stick. (I soon learned to keep my knees as far apart as possible!) Then, he put his hands in the air to signal that I was to take over. (No intercom in this little bird.) Coming out of that maneuver, I had a hard job orientating myself to try the left and right turns again. But I was a fast learner and finally caught on that in a turn, especially a steep turn, you had to pull back a little on the stick to keep the nose on the horizon. By the end of the hour, I was making some decent turns. Six dollars and one lesson down.

In the second lesson a week or so later, Barney added a real challenge as we prepared for another session of what he called "air work." Down at the end of the grass runway and in position for takeoff, he said, "You do the takeoff, and keep it going straight." Whoa! The Cub is a tail dragger, and until you get the tail up, you can't see a thing out the windshield—especially with someone blocking your view of not only the instrument panel, but also the windshield. Well, here goes as I shoved the throttle forward with my left hand. Almost immediately we were headed for the bushes! I pushed on the opposite rudder pedal, and guess what, we headed for more bushes in the other direction this time. Wow! How do you keep this thing going straight? We were doing "S" turns down the runway until we had enough speed to get off the ground. Amazing how docile the airplane becomes once off the ground and into the air.

Up at altitude, which in those days a 1,000 feet seemed awfully high, we leveled off at probably 2,000 feet or so.

"Okay," he said, "I'll demonstrate a poweroff stall." With that, he pulled the throttle back to idle, pulled the nose up steeply, and when the little bird protested with a shudder, he pushed the nose down and rammed the throttle forward as we leveled off. Now it was my turn. Could I do it? I better, or my knees were going to take another beating! I did all the wrong things a student does at first—pushed the nose down too soon before the airplane had completely stalled, then hauled back on the stick too abruptly before the airspeed indicator had come alive again. So, we practiced and practiced until I could fully stall the airplane and make a clean recovery. In those days, the FAA, then called the CAA, required spins as a part of the flight test to get a Private Pilot License. A "tailspin" is when the airplane is stalled with the power off, and the pilot must hold the stick all the way back in his lap and kick the rudder so that the plane pitches over into a rotating spin with the nose pointed straight down. After we landed and could communicate better, Barney said we would do spins next time around. O, joy! What's that going to be like? I went home and searched my CAA Maneuver Manual to read the section about spins. I hoped that would prepare me for what was ahead. But would there be another lesson? My fifty cents an hour fund was almost depleted. Boy! I didn't want to have to quit now when I was just getting the hang of flying. Maybe my friend would have some ideas of how I could continue flying lessons. Maybe he could teach me now that I had a few basics nailed.

I knew he often hung out at a hamburger shop on the town triangle, so I went there, plopped down on a stool next to him and made my pitch. I would work on his farm on Saturdays driving tractors or doing other odd jobs he needed most if he would give me flying lessons. By this time he knew that I was serious about learning to fly and I would not be denied. He munched on his hamburger for a few minutes while he thought about it, then said, "Okay, I'll pick you up this Saturday to go to the farm." Believe me, that made my day! Blue sky, here I come.

★ ★ ★ ★

HAYFIELD FLYING

To me, there is nothing like flying out of hayfields. The farmland of Northern Illinois is flat and provides excellent landing fields. When the hay crop got too high, we would simply move the airplane to a nearby recently mowed hayfield. Every field was a new challenge. Over the years, the experience I gained flying off hayfields taught me valuable short field techniques.

Anticipating that first Saturday of farm work, the prospect of more flight instruction occupied my every waking minute. I wasn't looking forward to the work—he might have me shoveling manure or something. I was focused on the flying at the end of the work day. I thought the week would never end. But it did, and off we went to the farm. The day went pretty fast, and in the late afternoon we drove to the hayfield where the Cub was tied down. It wasn't the prettiest airplane you ever saw, but I didn't much care; it was an airplane! It was a J-2 model Piper Cub, which meant that it was powered by a forty horsepower Continental four-cylinder engine. Those early model Pipers didn't have brakes, but they did have a steerable tail wheel which provided steering on the ground. It was a little rough-looking, but it looked good to me. I found out later that part of the preflight walk around was checking the fabric on the top of the wings and tail to see if there were any holes in the fabric. The fabric was old, and if a big enough bird landed on the top of the wing, it would

CAPT. DON H. BELDIN

split the fabric. This became my first introduction to doing fabric work. He always had a gallon can of fabric dope and some cloth to patch the hole. At one point I counted twenty-seven patches on the top of the right wing!

My farmer friend was not a flight instructor. In fact, he didn't even have a Private Pilot's License, but I didn't know that at the time. I guess somewhere along the line he had gotten someone to give him some basic flight instruction, much as he was doing for me. But he hadn't taken the written test or the flight test for a Private Pilot's License, so he was limited in what he could teach me. I already had practiced some of the basic air work maneuvers from the instruction I had at Hillcrest Airport, so about all he worked on with me were takeoffs and landings. He always crawled in the rear seat, which put me in the front seat; therefore I did all of my practice takeoffs and landings from the front seat. That became a significant factor later on when I was ready to solo.

Most all of the hayfields were planted in alfalfa hay. Alfalfa is a low growing plant, more like a vine. Farmers usually harvested about three crops of hay from a field during the summer. We had to carefully watch how long the alfalfa was getting each week so that we could move the airplane before it got too long. Sometimes it would get ahead of us, and it would be difficult to get airborne before the fence on the other end of the field. Not all hayfields were the same size. Some fields were square, and some were rectangular. My friend weighed at least 200 pounds, and I was a tall lanky kid weighing about 140 pounds. After I had soloed and had gotten some flight experience, I was the one who was elected to fly the airplane out if the hay had gotten too long. Some of those flights just barely made it over the hayfield fence because the long hay kept the airplane from gaining enough airspeed to get in the air.

Throughout that summer I accumulated about ten or fifteen hours of flight time. My takeoffs and landings were coming right along, and I wondered if I was good enough to solo. My personal goal was to solo before the winter weather set in and curtailed most of our flying. But would my friend trust me with his airplane even if he thought I was ready to solo? I could only hope he would!

★ ★ ★ ★ ★

FIRST SOLO

Every student pilot looks forward with mixed emotions to the day the instructor says, "Okay, if you make three near perfect takeoffs and landings today, I'm going to let you solo." Oh boy! The long-awaited day has finally come. Now if I can only plant it on the end of the runway three times in a row, he'll turn me loose for my first solo. Mentally you go over every detail of the upcoming pre-solo flight—keep it going straight down the runway—climb to 400 feet—make a coordinated left turn—climb to 600 feet—make another ninety degree left turn—level off and maintain altitude as you parallel the runway on the downwind leg—throttle back as you pass the end of the runway just off your left wing—make a left turn to the base leg of the traffic pattern—don't forget to advance the throttle momentarily to clear the engine—turn onto final maintain sixty-five mph indicated airspeed as you approach the runway threshold—don't level off too high—over the runway gradually pull the nose up into a three point position—keep the stick in your lap as you gently touchdown on the runway. Yep, that's all there is to it—that is IF I can keep everything in sequence! A little mental pep talk, and I'm ready to go!

That Sunday morning dawned with an overcast sky. I wondered if we would be able to fly that afternoon as it looked like rain. My Sunday morning job at our church was to ring the big bell in the church belfry. It may be old-fashioned now, but there is just something about the pealing of a church bell on Sunday morning that still warms my heart.

All through Sunday school and church, mentally I was out at the hayfield reliving another flying lesson. I had no idea my farmer instructor thought I was ready to solo. You have to remember that our "airport" was nothing but a hayfield with no marked runway. We just took off in whatever direction the wind was blowing, and that was our "runway" for the day. You always had a fence to clear, which wasn't much of a problem unless the current mowed hayfield was a bit small.

I gulped down my dinner, and off I went on my bike to catch my ride to the "airport." Boy, the weather didn't look all that great, but I figured if we could stay under the overcast, then maybe we could get a thirty-minute flight in. By this time, I had progressed to practicing takeoffs and landings, so if we had at least a 1,000 foot ceiling, we would be okay.

In the mid-forties, flying wasn't that far removed from the barnstorming era, and regulations were minimal. But out in the hayfields of Northern Illinois, who cared about regulations? Because he had always flown his Cub alone, my friend flew it from the rear seat, which was correct. So, all of the instruction he gave me was from the back with me flying from the front seat. That suited me just fine because I could see over the nose better and the instrument panel was right in front of me. As we prepared to fly, he uttered those long-anticipated words, "If you make three good takeoffs and landings, I may let you take it around the patch by yourself." The challenge was on. "However," he continued, "you will have to fly it from the rear seat, and that might be a problem. Maybe we could strap a sack of oats in the rear seat so you could fly it from the front seat." He was dead serious, but we lacked the sack of oats. I quickly assured him that I was sure I could handle it from the rear seat because my first flight instruction at Hillcrest Airport was from the rear seat. I think he figured

I would botch at least one of the landings and he would be off the hook.

We took off, and I did the three takeoffs and landings without a hitch. True to his promise, he got out, I climbed to the back seat, and he swung the prop to restart the engine. I don't think I'll ever forget the feeling as I taxied down to the end of the hayfield for takeoff. Boy, that instrument panel seemed like a long ways away. And that empty front seat reminded me that a successful solo flight was entirely up to me. I was both exhilarated and slightly fearful. I lined up with the imaginary runway and began the takeoff roll. The Cub leaped into the air with just a 140 pound pilot and climbed like a homesick angel. Before I knew it, I was into that solid overcast, but quickly pushed forward on the stick to get the nose down and out of that white stuff. I turned to the downwind nervously planning my approach and landing. Because I was higher than our normal 600 foot pattern, I was too high as I turned onto final approach. Yep, you guessed it—I came across the fence too high with the prospect of landing in two hayfields to the north. I'm sure my friend was watching wondering if his Cub would be worth rebuilding if I didn't get it down successfully.

I applied full power for the go-around and this time took a quick look at the altimeter and leveled off at 600 feet. Things looked more promising this time and final approach brought me across the fence to a smooth three point landing. Wow! I did it! I actually flew it all by myself! Talk about a confidence-builder. By this time there were several people who had stopped by to watch, and they all congratulated me.

I could hardly wait to tell my parents and my little sister that I had soloed. Mom was taking a Sunday afternoon nap when I bounded into the house, and Dad was upstairs in his study preparing his sermon for the evening service. I think they received my news with mixed emotions—happy for my achievement, but concerned that their little boy was not confined to riding a bike but was now flying airplanes. My dear Mom always said that when I should have just been riding my bike, I was driving a car, and when I should have been driving a car, I was flying airplanes. She also told me that I contributed largely to the premature gray hair that was appearing in her waist length hair. And looking back on my teen years, I have to admit she was probably right.

But there is a sequel to this first solo experience. I could hardly wait to tell my buddies at high school that I had soloed. I suggested to my closest friend that after school we ride our bikes out to see the Piper Cub I had flown on Sunday afternoon. We rode the three miles to the hayfield where the Cub was parked. It was a beautiful sunny fall afternoon. No one was around. I was suddenly gripped by the urge to fly it around the field. We untied the airplane, got it started and off we went with my friend as my passenger. Looking back on it now, I cannot believe I took that airplane for a ride without permission! I cannot believe that on my second solo hop I flew my first passenger! But then, youth has no fear, and I certainly didn't. My guardian angel had his work cut out for him starting that day.

A SUMMER ADVENTURE

School was out. I had just finished my junior year, and the summer was ahead. My favorite class that year was Typing II. My teacher was a twenty-one-year-old first-year teacher named Patrica Gibson. I think she was impressed that at age seventeen I was learning to fly. I was a pretty good typist by then, easily typing forty or more words per minute, so I excelled in her class. If I finished the class assignment, I would type a little note, take it up to her desk, and she would write something funny on it. We went to football games together with a carload of kids, then a few bowling dates with a gang from school. It was all very innocent.

Pat had to finish her college degree by attending summer school. The college was only eighty miles away, and after exchanging a few letters, I decided I'd drive up to see her. I got permission to use the family car on some pretext, and off I went. I was about twenty miles from the college town in Wisconsin when I passed an airport just outside of Janesville. Whoa! Maybe I could rent an airplane and fly up to this small college town. It would be a lot more impressive. So I turned in and was able to rent a former Army artillery spotter plane—a two place tandem Taylorcraft L2M with the glass windows all around the back of the cabin. I never had flown one before, but it couldn't be much different than a Cub. I still only had a student permit, not a Private Pilots License.

In about twenty minutes flight time, the town came into view. Pat was living in a sorority house with a main street address. I figured if I picked out the main street running through downtown and followed it to the college campus, I could spot the house. So, I dropped down to about a hundred feet, flew up West Main Street and thought I spotted the sorority house. Pull up, make a 180, and drop back down to fly by the house again. Just as I thought! My low pass had shaken some of the girls out of the house, and as I flew by I spotted Pat out on the lawn. Now, find a good hayfield close to the edge of town with a farmhouse nearby so I could make a phone call. East of town I found a hayfield that looked like it was long enough for the T-Craft. After all, the L2M had spoilers on the wing which, when engaged by a handle on the right side of the cockpit, would kill the lift and allow you to land on short fields.

The landing went okay, and I shut down in the corner of the field nearest the farmhouse. I was met by the farmer's son, who was home on furlough from the Army. I asked if I could use the telephone, and he walked me to the house. From our correspondence, I had the address and telephone number of the sorority house. When Pat came to the phone, I told her approximately where I was and suggested she come out. She said she would, but she would have to walk. Being a small town, it was probably only two or three miles.

As the soldier and I walked back out to the airplane, I noticed that some kids that lived nearby had arrived. As we stood by the airplane, the farm boy asked how much would I take to give him a ride. I thought a minute, then said a dollar. And with that he produced the dollar which I stuffed into my pocket. The kids around us were in awe and heard the conversation. I cranked up and took off. This would be a great opportunity to observe the progress of Pat as she walked east down Main Street. So his ride consisted of a hundred foot low pass up the left side of Main Street looking for someone walking, and sure enough, there she was waving. Back to the hayfield landing. To my amazement, these kids were waving dollar bills saying they wanted a ride, too. So for the next hour I buckled one kid after another in the back seat, pocketed their dollars and took off to follow the progress of Pat. She was making progress, and when she was almost to the farm, I landed and ended my passenger hopping enterprise. My pockets were stuffed with dollar bills, enough to pay for the rental of the airplane and some besides.

Pat finally arrived at the farm, and the trusting soul that she was, climbed in the back seat, and we were off to the Janesville Airport to refuel. An idea had been hatching in my mind as I was giving rides. I was having a ball, so why end it at the Janesville airport where I rented the airplane? After all, I had my high school typing teacher in the back seat to impress. Why not fly on down to my hometown, only sixty miles away? I thought it was a good idea—I could afford to rent the T-Craft for another hour or so. So Warren, ready or not, here we come!

As we approached the northeast side of town, I decided to buzz a friend's auto body shop. Nose down with full throttle, we buzzed across the roof of his building. And that started it all. Back to when I was a pre-teen, my favorite radio program at 5:45 every night was Captain Midnight. I rarely ever missed it. The program always started with Captain Midnight banking in a tight turn around a clock tower as it struck midnight. There was a water tower by the library near the downtown stores that was 100 feet high. As I was learning to fly, I vowed that someday I would do a Captain Midnight and fly around that water tower! Well, there it was dead ahead. Now's my chance. The big letters "Warren" beckoned, so around we went right over downtown. Believe me, I heard about it later, but at the time no one knew who was flying that "red airplane." The fun was just beginning. I buzzed everyone I knew. Inadvertently in one of my low passes on the west side of town, I flew low over a pasture where a small dairy herd was grazing. The herd belonged to Mr. Wilson who sold milk door to door. In fact, it was he that I had worked for peddling milk every morning a few years before. My presence just over their heads scared them, and they stampeded through two fences into another farmer's field! Whoops! Sorry about that, although I didn't know it at the time.

The mayor owned the local farm implement business, and his phone suddenly started ringing off the wall! There were many elderly widows in Warren, and all that low flying over town scared them half to death. They were sure that airplane was going to crash into their roofs. They demanded that he do something, anything!

In our little farm community, there were five of us that flew—three farmers, the DeKalb Corn Plant manager, and myself. One of those men farmed three miles south of town. He had an airplane and a airstrip on his farm. *Let's go and see what's going on down on the farm,* I thought. He was just building a T-hangar near the barnyard, and I saw a half dozen men nailing on the metal roof. Again, nose down, throttle forward, and buzz across the roof. I heard later that it scared one elderly man so that he began to slide down the roof heading for the edge, but fortunately someone grabbed him before he went over the edge.

I had just about buzzed everyone I could think of as I climbed for some altitude and headed back toward town. Well, bless my soul, who should I see at the edge of town but a man hoeing his garden. Could it be the town constable? It was, and he was always flagging me down for driving too fast through town. It's payback time! As I headed down toward him, I saw him look up with hoe in hand at the airplane headed toward him and just as I pulled up I saw him throw his hoe and dive face down in the dirt. That had to be the funniest thing I had ever seen! Couldn't stop laughing. Let's do it again! Back down from the other direction this time heading toward the figure that was standing brushing off his clothes. He heard the airplane and saw it heading down toward him again. As I pulled up, I saw this poor soul dive flat out in the dirt again. I guess even a small airplane looks pretty big coming at you at fifty feet. I'm ashamed now to say that I made that old man kiss the dirt three times that day! And me the preacher's son! Well, you know what they say about preacher's kids. I certainly personified it that day.

Time was up, so I headed back for Janesville. In those days, cruising altitude was 500 feet. As we headed northeast out of town, I noticed a tractor pulling a load of hay in from the field. Immediately I knew this was the farm of a high school buddy. I must give him his thrill for the day, so again, nose down, throttle full forward, the target was that load of hay. There was a man standing on the top of the hay load leaning on his pitchfork. He must have heard the engine, or he may have been facing my direction. Just before I zoomed across the hay load, I saw him bail out off the load. Make a mental note not to admit to his son that it was me that buzzed him that summer afternoon.

On the flight back, I decided to drop into an airport midway back to Janesville to get some fuel. I had flown off this airstrip before. The farm buildings on the approach end to the grass runway required you to fly to the right of the barn and silo, then bank to the left to line up with the runway. Remember, this former artillery spotter airplane had spoilers built into the top of the wing. Because I was a little high as I came across the end of the runway, I decided to use the spoilers to kill the lift which would cause the airplane to lose altitude and mush to a touch down. As I said, I was a little high, and we dropped in to a hard landing. All of a sudden, the right wing dropped down the wingtip touching the ground, and the airplane skidding around in a 180. In other words, we stopped heading in the direction we had just come from! Oh boy! I thought I'd wrecked this rented airplane! When I got out, I realized what had happened. The shock absorber cord on the right landing gear had broken because of the hard landing. (A shock cord was a series of rubber band covered with nylon.) Now what do I do? They say necessity is the mother of invention. There were people standing around— did they see the landing? Someone suggested that I wind a clothes line rope around the place where the shock cord had been as a temporary repair. Good idea. I got someone to drive me to the nearest hardware store, and I bought fifty feet of clothesline rope. Back at the airport, some guys held the wing up while I wrapped the rope around the landing gear. Bingo! Just like new! So I refueled and took off.

The grass runways of Janesville airport came into view, and with an impressive landing we ended a most enjoyable day. When I walked into the airport office, I carried the broken shock cord and laid it on his desk. He stood right up to look out the front windows and said, "Where's the airplane?" I told him what had happened and how I did a temporary repair to fly it home, and he broke into laughter, probably mostly from relief. It had been an exciting day, but I'm sure I gave my guardian angel a real workout. As for Pat, I assumed she was enjoying her ride since she didn't upchuck down the back of my neck!

★ ★ ★ ★ ★ ★ ★

RELIVING THOSE BARN STORMING DAYS

The barnstorming era was long gone, but one summer four of us found ourselves reliving it every Sunday afternoon. My farmer friend had his forty-horsepowered Cub that I had soloed in. Another pilot from a nearby town had a forty-horse-powered Taylorcraft, and another forty-horsepowered T-Craft was owned by a farmer who planned to learn how to fly. Since he hadn't started flying lessons, and probably wouldn't any time soon, he asked me to fly him around. That was a big plus for me because I could fly his airplane and it didn't cost me a dime.

Pilots are funny creatures—they look for excuses to fly. One Sunday afternoon we decided to crank up the three air-planes and fly down to Lena, another farm town close by. By this time I had accumulated nearly 100 hours of flight time, much of it practicing loops and spins. (It's not easy to loop a forty hp airplane, but if you dove it and got enough airspeed it would go all the way around the loop.) We circled town looking for a recently mowed hayfield along side a highway where we could land. Once the other two airplanes were on the ground, I did the only two aerobatics I knew how to do, and that the airplane could handle. Yep, you guessed it, loops and spins. Usually a loop and a spin were enough to attract some attention. The airplanes sitting in the hayfield along side the highway also attracted passing motorists.

The hayfield was ideal because it was right at the edge of town. By the time I landed there was a line of cars parked on the side of the road. As curious people gathered around the three airplanes looking and asking questions, inevitably someone would ask if they could get a ride. The answer of course, was sure—for five bucks. And from that point on, all three of us got very busy for the rest of the afternoon giving airplane rides. We didn't make a lot, but it was enough to pay for the fuel and a little for our pockets.

This was what the pilots of the twenties and early thirties did—tour towns across the country giving rides out of whatever field was available near a highway. It was a gypsy kind of life—sleeping under the wing at night, hustling to the next town in the morning, pick out a landing field, set up the "AIRPLANE RIDES" signs, and get ready for another day of hard flying. Why did they do it? Well, they loved to fly and flying jobs were hard to find. Beyond that, the money kept the airplane flying and kept pilots in hamburgers and hot dogs. But it was a romantic lifestyle.

One passenger who climbed into the seat next to me in that forty-horsepowered Taylorcraft was the dentist in town. He was a rather large passenger. In fact, if memory serves me correctly, it was a struggle to get the seat belt around him. He sucked in his gut, and we got it latched and taxied to the north end of the field. This was summertime, and Illinois afternoons get rather downright hot. There was very little breeze to help get the airplane in the air within the confines of the hayfield fences. Midway in our takeoff I began to doubt we were going to clear the fence that was coming up all too fast. To complicate the situation, there were two small trees at the fence line. Fortunately, the trees were not really close together, but when you know you're not going to clear them, they look VERY close together. I had no choice—I'd be able to clear the fence but not the trees. What do you do in that case? You fly between them! And that's exactly what I did. We cleared the fence by inches and went between the two trees. We made it between them, but not by much. I've often wondered what the dentist thought as he saw the two trees go by the windows at eye level! Maybe he thought that was part of our act. Coolheaded as I appeared on the outside, I just acted like this was routine and gave him his ride. He didn't know it, but he got his five bucks worth that day. The rest of the afternoon I made sure I got the light weights. Later, I walked down to see how close those trees were together. I paced it off and it was about fifty feet. The T-craft wing span is thirty-six feet. You do the math.

As I said, we looked for excuses to fly, and this was one way to spend a summer afternoon. The forties were still free and easy times when flying was a sport and not encumbered with a lot of restrictive regulations. Those were truly the *good ol' days!*

★ ★ ★ ★ ★ ★ ★ ★

HOW MUCH WAS THAT AIRPLANE?

It was 1946. The war was over, and the economy was booming. The government had a glut of war surplus airplanes ranging from training aircraft to fighter and bomber airplanes. A government agency had been established called the Reconstruction Finance Corporation (F) to market some of these surplus airplanes to the civilian market. I heard about this and somehow got on their mailing list. Every week the RFC mailed out lists of airplanes for sale. I was interested in one airplane—the Boeing-built Stearman. This was one of several primary trainers that were used to teach men in the Air Corps how to fly. It was an open cockpit biplane with a 220 hp Continental seven-cylinder radial engine up front. The first batch that was offered was priced at $2,750 each. Even at that price it was a bargain because the government paid about $10,000 per airplane. But, it was way out of financial reach for an eighteen-year-old. So week by week I watched the price come down with every mailing. What was happening was they would sell off a bunch at the published price, sales would drop as the airplanes were picked over, and then they would lower the price. I watched the price drop to $2,500, then $2,250, then $2,000, and so on until the price got down to a $1,000. Still too much for me, but it really got my attention when it went down to $500! Wow, I thought as I looked for a way to come up with $500. When I received the next mailing, they had lowered the price for a Stearman biplane down to an astounding $250. You can believe that I was on the next train to Oklahoma City with a $250 cashier's check in my pocket! It never occurred to me that at that price they couldn't be flyable airplanes.

It was an all-night train ride, but I didn't get much sleep. The airplanes were located at Cimmorron Air Base west of Oklahoma City. The train arrived in Okie City in the morning, and I hitch-hiked out to the air base at Yukon, Oklahoma. At the administration building they showed me a book that listed all the Stearmans that were still available with total airframe and engine times since overhaul. I picked out ten airplanes that looked promising by their location on the airbase. A military guard took me out in a jeep to look at the airplanes I had selected. The first one on my list looked like it had been through the war and back! The fabric was hanging in shreds, and it was immediately apparent that that bird wouldn't fly. Eight other airplanes on my list were in like condition. By this time, it dawned on me that the crop of flyable airplanes had already been picked over. At $250, what could you expect?

I had one last airplane on my list. I gave the guard the location, and he said, "Oh, I think that's that old dog over in the northwest corner. You don't want to go see it, do you?"

My answer was, "I've come 750 miles, so I might as well take the time to look at one more." So off we went.

When we drove up in front of the airplane I couldn't believe my eyes. There sat a beautiful yellow Stearman with Navy markings on it, poised as if ready to fly. I walked around it, thumped on the fabric in strategic places, and it was as tight as a snare drum. I hopped into the jeep and said, "Get me back to the Ad building quick!" I was afraid that someone else might be getting a bill of sale on that airplane ahead of me. But I was in time, and they gave me a bill of sale on Boeing 07481. It was November 21, 1946, and I was now the proud owner of my first airplane.

I was standing near one of the hangars when I saw them pull the airplane into the hangar. By this time it was about four o'clock, and one of the mechanics came over and told me that they wouldn't be able to get it ready until the next morning. When these surplus airplanes were flown in and put in storage, the engines were drained of oil and a pickling solution was pumped in to preserve them. What that $250 bought me was not only the airplane but fresh engine oil in the oil tank and forty-six gallons of fuel. As I looked from a distance at that airplane it looked huge compared to the Cubs and T-crafts I had been flying. In fact, the largest airplanes I had flown up to then were sixty-five horse-powered birds. Sitting in front of the hangar was an open cockpit biplane with a 220 hp engine up front! I had never had a ride in an open cockpit airplane, let alone flown one! An official check-out would have been good, but that wasn't included in the selling price. Their philosophy was, "You bought it, you fly it out of here!"

I caught a ride to the nearby town and got a $3 room in the only hotel on Main Street. I relived the day over and over in my mind and tossed and turned until morning light. A quick breakfast at a local diner, and I was hitch-hiking on the highway leading to Cimmorron Air Base. I was early, so I had to wait awhile as they prepared *my* Stearman for flight. By mid-morning it rolled out of the hangar ready to fly. I had prepared for this flight by bringing my A-2 leather flight jacket, a flannel shirt, two pair of pants, leather gloves, and a pair of fleece-lined Army sky boots. I thought I was well prepared for the November weather up north. Little did I realize how cold you get in an open cockpit airplane in November.

I climbed in the rear cockpit where the pilot normally sits to fly, looked around to become familiar with where things were, and motioned for a mechanic to wind me up. On the

Stearman there was an inertia starter on the left side and just behind the engine. You inserted a crank and began winding up the weighted flywheel. Then, you pulled on a handle to engage the starter to the engine. If you were in luck, the engine would start the first time. It did, and now it was show time—time to prove I was up to the challenge. I taxied to the runway and lined up for takeoff. With my courage screwed all the way up, I pushed the throttle forward and began the takeoff roll. My first thrill was just ahead.

THE THRILL OF OPEN COCKPIT FLYING

The Stearman rose gently from the runway. I couldn't believe I was already in the air. I had popped the stick forward after beginning the takeoff roll to get the tail up to level flight, but I didn't get the tail quite high enough. In a slightly tail low position it just said, "I'm ready," and it flew off on its own. I got a real thrill when I made my first turn. Sitting in that open cockpit with my shoulders and head sticking up in the breeze, I was looking at nothing but space as I banked in a left turn. I was use to being encapsulated in a cabin with sides and windows surrounding me. This was certainly a new experience flying an open cockpit biplane.

Another new experience was flying off of hard surface runways. I climbed to altitude and took an easterly heading for Oklahoma City. I needed to buy some navigation charts to get me to Illinois. I was a bit nervous about the upcoming landing, my first in a Stearman, at Okie City International Airport. All of our flying was either off grass runways or hayfields. There is a big difference. I had my education brought up to date while talking with a pilot that had learned to fly in Stearmans. He gave me some valuable advice before I left home. He said, "That narrow gear on a Stearman will give you a hair-raising ride if it ever does a ground loop. If you let the airplane stray five degrees off the centerline, you probably will lose it. If you let it move to ten degrees from straight ahead you have lost it!" So with his words ringing in my ears, I lined up with the runway at Oklahoma City Airport and made my first Stearman landing without incident. Believe me, I was on those brakes and rudder pedals making sure I kept it right on the runway centerline.

I got my aeronautical charts and took off for Tulsa where I planned to overnight with a friend at Spartan School of Aeronautics. I spent the evening going over my charts and laying out my course to Illinois. There were no navigation radios in our kind of airplanes—you flew strictly by watching for landmarks to come up on or near the penciled line that you had drawn between your departure and arrival destination. It was called pilotage. All in all, I felt pretty good about the Stearman since I had about two hours already logged so far and two successful landings. Now, get a little shut eye for the 700-mile flight to Illinois.

When I awoke, I heard the wind blowing a gale. Of course, the wind always blows in Oklahoma, but this sounded much stronger than yesterday. And it was! About twenty-five to thirty mph with gusts. But the good thing was that it was blowing out of the south, and I was flying northeast. I'd get a good tailwind out of this one. So I stowed my maps inside the cockpit and cranked up. Taxiing downwind to the active runway was a challenge in itself. The wind blowing on the tail plastered the rudder over to one side and there was no way I could push it back to neutral with the rudder pedals. I didn't bother with a run-up—I just wanted to get this bird in the air before the wind flipped me over while on the ground. A quick turn onto the runway and full throttle—I was in the air in a couple hundred feet. I had climbed to a thousand feet before I reached the end of the runway. A left turn to my northeast heading, and it was goodbye Tulsa—that airport disappeared out of sight in a matter of minutes. I got my first chart out and started navigating by landmarks.

Thirty minutes into the flight, I didn't have the foggiest idea of where I was. The quartering tailwind was pushing me faster than I could change maps. Now don't get me wrong. The Stearman is normally a ninety mph airplane. But add that twenty-five or thirty mph tail wind, and I was cruising! So what do you do when you don't know where you are? One thing we used to do was fly over to the nearest town and drop down to read the name of the town off the large letters on the water tower. Every town had a water tower, and it was a good way to get your bearings. But I didn't have to do that. Just off to my left I spotted some men in a corner of a Missouri field shredding corn. Conveniently there was a hayfield next to them, so I landed and taxied up to the fence. I hopped out but left the engine idling, and walked over to one of the men who was wide-eyed in unbelief. With all my flying gear on I must have looked like I just landed from Mars! "Where am I?" I asked as I showed him the map. He'd never seen an aeronautical map before, but finally he found the nearby town. The strong south wind had blown me about thirty miles west of my intended course. I thanked him, jumped back in the airplane and took off. I imagine those men had something to talk about at the local barbershop that Saturday.

Back in the air I made a course correction to compensate for the wind drift and my landmarks started coming up—fly between two towns with a major highway connecting them—find that river that my course intersects at the big bend—fly parallel to the double railroad tracks leading out of that town—and so on mile after mile.

I was getting low on fuel as the Mississippi River and Davenport, Iowa, showed up on the nose. It had been a long day, and it would soon be dark, so I decided to stay overnight. I would have a much shorter hop in the morning to my destination of Warren, Illinois. Seventy-five miles and I would be home! By this time I had about seven hours flight time in the Stearman and was feeling quite comfortable with this new bird. So far the weather had been good and flying an open cockpit airplane had been quite comfortable with the southern wind. I didn't know it then, but the next day would bring a new element into the trip—weather.

The next morning dawned bright and sunny but bitterly cold! I was glad I had prepared by bringing along some warm clothing. It was going to be a longer flight than I thought. The wind had switched around to the north which meant I would have a headwind the rest of the way. No matter, I would be warm with my helmet and goggles, gloves, two shirts, two pairs of pants, fleece lined Army ski boots, and my leather A-2 flight jacket. Boy was I wrong!

As soon as I took off from Davenport and flew across the mighty Mississippi, I knew this was going to be a *cold* ride! Because of the headwind I thought I'd never get across that river to the Illinois side. But I did, and there was something comforting about being back over land again. I shuddered to think of having an engine failure and having to ditch this kind of airplane in that muddy Mississippi. Already the only exposed part of my face—my mouth—was suffering. My fleece lined ski boots weren't doing their job either. I started stomping my feet on the floor board runners in the hope of keeping some warm blood circulating. My gloved right hand was wrapped around the control stick as I now followed familiar landmarks leading me home. I thought this leg of the flight would never end! Was I making any progress? It almost looked like cars and trucks on the highway were going faster than I was. That had happened to me a few years earlier when I flew a forty-hp Cub I had soloed in up from Tulsa. I had taken off from Vandalia, Missouri, for Marshall, Missouri, a distance of thirty miles. Flying right alongside a four-lane highway, I saw semi-trucks come from behind, pass me, and disappear ahead as I bucked a strong headwind. It took me two hours to go thirty miles! Fifteen mph in an airplane?! It happens when you only have forty horses pulling you and a strong headwind.

Finally, I saw the water tower of Warren appear over the nose. I would land in the hayfield on the northeast edge of town. Two of my pilot friends in town knew that I had gone down to Oklahoma to pick up a Stearman, so they were looking for me. I made two circles around town (I was so cold by now that a few minutes more wouldn't matter) and landed in the hayfield. I taxied up to the corner where the Cub was tied down and shut down. Try as I might, I could not get out of that airplane! The fingers of my right hand were so cold I had to pry them off the control stick. I was so cold and my joints were so stiff I could not push myself up far enough to get my elbows on the cockpit rim and stand on the seat to put my left leg over the cockpit side and onto the wing walk. I struggled for a couple of minutes to no avail until my two friends arrived. It took both of them under each armpit to lift me up and help me out of the airplane. One of these guys was the owner of the auto body shop that was only a block away. Once inside his shop I stood by his pot bellied stove that was roaring hot, and literally shook for thirty minutes. I couldn't say a word because my teeth were doing a tap dance! I had never been as cold before or since. But all of that was soon forgotten as I related my story to them that day, and now to you, dear reader.

★ ★ ★ ★ ★ ★ ★ ★ ★ ★ ★

HEY! WAIT FOR ME

A few days after arriving from Oklahoma, I could no longer stifle the urge to get back in the cockpit and do a little flying. I needed fuel, so I took off from the hayfield and flew three miles down to a nearby farm that had an airstrip. This was the farm that I buzzed when they were just building the T-hangar. I landed and taxied up to the end of the T-hangar where the fuel pump was and shut down. The little office was locked, so I checked around the hangar, but no one was in sight. I looked in the barn that was nearby, but not a soul was anywhere around. After waiting for a short time, I decided to crank up and leave. Now, you need to get a mental picture of the scene. My Stearman was parked at the end of the T-hangar headed south. About two hundred feet straight ahead was the back of a building used to house farm machinery. About one hundred feet or so the right there was a straw stack standing in the fence corner at the edge of an open area. In the center of this open space there was a light pole carrying electricity to the hangar. This was in November, so the roughness of the ground had been frozen hard.

I had come up with my own system of starting the airplane when by myself. The inertia starter had to be cranked to get it spinning, then pull the clutch T-handle to engage it to the engine. If I was alone I would put my right foot on the wing next to the side of the fuselage and my left foot down on the landing gear tire. This put me in reasonably good po-

CAPT. DON H. BELDIN

sition to insert the crank and start winding up the inertia starter flywheel. I turned the magneto switch to on, cracked the throttle just a tad above idle, assumed the position, and started cranking. Believe me when I say that you were good for only one wind up because of the energy it took to get that internal flywheel spinning. Well, you guessed it—it turned the engine over alright, but it didn't start! I reached around with my right arm and without looking, gave the throttle lever a little forward nudge. By now I was winded, so I decided to stand on the landing gear tire with both feet which would put me directly in front of the crank. Wind it up again, pull the handle to engage the starter to the engine, and after a few turns the engine fired up. I wasn't prepared for what happened next, and what was going to happen during the next few minutes!

Immediately the airplane started to move forward—I had given it more throttle than I thought. Remember, I'm standing with both feet on the wheel. When the airplane started to move it threw me off onto the ground. I was lying on my back, and I saw the wing pass over me, then the tail. My airplane was going off without me! I got right up and started chasing it. Because it was November, I was wearing two of everything to keep warm. Yep, I even had on those fleeced lined ski boots, all of which impeded my ability to run even though the airplane wasn't moving fast.

I did catch up to it once, and while running got between the tail and the wing. I was trying to hoist myself up on the lower wing to get into the cockpit, but slipped and fell. Again, the tail passed over me. On my feet again to resume the chase. It was headed right for that farm building. I was gaining on it again, but a clump of frozen turf caused the airplane to turn ninety degrees to the right. Now disaster was really threatening because it was headed right for the straw stack. A hot engine and straw don't mix. It doesn't take a rocket scientist to figure out that fire would envelope the stack and my $250 airplane with it! I was still pursuing the chase, and I almost caught up with it again, but just before it got to the straw stack another frozen turf caught the right wheel and the airplane made a complete 180 degree turn. Whoa! Now this thing is going to chase me! I'll never forget seeing that nine foot metal Hartzel prop coming toward me like a giant meat cleaver. By this time I was really winded from the chase, but adrenaline kicked in and I was off like a Olympic sprinter, glancing over my shoulder to make sure my airplane wasn't gaining on me. I saw that the uneven turf had gotten the airplane doing 360s in the open yard. It made three circles each one getting closer to that utility pole. Finally the left wings hit the 10 inch pole breaking it off like a toothpick. The airplane pivoted around one more time, and this time the three-foot-tall stub went up between the landing gear. When the prop hit that stub, you would have thought there was a saw mill on the property! Chips flew everywhere as the prop chewed through what was left of the utility pole! And there she sat—engine running, but at least it wasn't moving. I ran up to the side, reached in the cockpit and just turned the switch off. I fell back on the ground, my lungs burning from the cold air. I was lying there trying to get my breath when the untimely arrival of the farmer jolted me back to reality. Boy, was he mad! I knew him well because we were fellow pilots. But what upset him so was not the damage to the left wings of my airplane, but the bro-ken utility pole with the sagging wires. Instead of consoling me, he issued a verbally spiced ultimatum. "Get this airplane out of here by five o'clock or you'll be in real trouble." Being young I conjured up the worst case scenario—he would con-fiscate my airplane.

I don't remember how I got to town, but I immediately went to the auto body shop and told my buddy what had happened. Together we drove out to the airstrip and there sat my airplane with a bent prop and the impression of the util-ity pole in the leading edge of the top and bottom of the left wing. He had some wrenches, so we pulled the prop off and took it back to his shop. The prop had a slight bend in both blades, so to straighten the blades we wedged them into the crotch of a tree by the shop and put our weight on the other end to bend it back to straight. That done, we saw that one blade had a part of the tip broken off. We took some measurements, cut the same amount off the other blade with a hacksaw, and rounded it off with his grinder. He had some black paint in his spray gun, so he shot the blades and it looked like it had just come out of a prop overhaul shop.

We were back out at the airstrip at four o'clock. My deadline was an hour away. We put the prop back on, and I was cranking it up just before five o'clock. I wasn't worried about the pole imprint in the two wings because it had only broken the nose ribs and bent the metal leading edge, but the spars on both wings were okay. The engine seemed to run okay, so I taxied down to the end of the airstrip that had been laid out between farm crops. I gave it full throttle and started the takeoff. It just wasn't accelerating normally so I held it on the ground, and as the fence loomed ahead, I hauled back on the stick. The airplane staggered over the fence, but sagged down on the other side. Now, the next field was a corn field that hadn't been picked yet. I was headed in the same direction as the rows of corn, and as the airplane sagged down after clearing the fence, the landing gear and prop started hitting the tops of the corn stalks. I picked two rows of corn halfway down the field before I got enough airspeed for the airplane to climb. With that bit of crisis over, I looked inside the cockpit at my instrument panel. It was shaking so badly that I could not read the engine rpm gage. Then I got a real shock when I looked out at my right wing tip. It was vibrating what appeared then to be six inches both ways—this airplane was about to shake itself apart! Now I was really scared. I spotted a hayfield just beyond the corn field, and plunked it down to a safe landing. In spite of the appearance and our careful calculations, the prop was way out of balance. If I had tried to fly any further I'm sure the engine bolts would have broken and the engine would have fallen off. A crash would have been inevitable. Again, I had succeeded in overworking my guardian angel. I can visualize him now hanging on like a barnstorming wing walker protecting me for future divine purposes. Thank you, Lord!

✱ ✱ ✱ ✱ ✱ ✱ ✱ ✱ ✱ ✱ ✱ ✱
TWENTY EXCITING MINUTES IN THE VULTEE BT-13

About the time I purchased a fly-away Stearman open cockpit biplane for $250, pilots I knew had also bought P-38s, twin engine fighter aircrafts, for $1,200 to $1,500. The farmer who owned the forty-horsepower T-craft, but didn't know how to fly, bought a Vultee BT-13 for $500. Somebody flew it to his farm, and it was parked in the corner of a field near the farmhouse.

One day I got a call from him wanting to know if I would come down and fly his BT-13. My first question was, "do you have any aviation fuel?" He assured me he did, so I agreed to meet him at the farm the next Saturday. The BT-13 was a basic trainer during the war. Air Corp pilots learned to fly in primary trainers like the Stearman (PT-17), then went on to basic training in the BT-13, then to advanced training in the AT-6, or in the case of bomber pilots, the twin engine Cessna AT-50, or the Beech AT-11. The BT-13, built by Consolidated Vultee Aircraft Company, was known as the Vultee Vibrator. It was a low wing all metal airplane, had a 450-hp Pratt & Whitney nine-cylinder radial engine up front, a fixed landing gear, a sliding canopy, and tandem seating for the pilot up front and instructor in the back cockpit. There were

BT-13s at Cimmorran Air Base where I found the Stearman, and I always thought I would like to fly one. Now I had my chance!

I drove down to my friend's farm the next Saturday and saw the BT-13 for the first time. He said he had fueled the airplane and it was ready to go. It was parked in the corner of a forty-acre square field that bordered the road in front of the farmhouse. I knew it would be tight, but I figured if I held the brakes, cranked in some flaps, and got that big "450" revving up, I could make it. But first I just wanted to sit in the front cockpit and get acquainted with the BT-13. Finally, I was ready to fire it up. It had an inertia starter like my Stearman, only you didn't have to have someone get it spinning with a crank—it had an electric motor to wind it up. A flick of a switch to get it spinning and a flick of another switch to engage it, and the prop started turning. I did it! I got the engine started! Now the moment of truth.

My friend climbed into the rear cockpit, and we put on the intercom headsets and started to taxi to the far corner of this forty-acre field. Run up went okay, although I had never been in an airplane with so many instruments staring me in the face. No matter, all I needed was the airspeed, altimeter, and engine rpm gauges, and I had located them on the panel. Off we went into the wild blue yonder! As I write this, I can't believe I did this. But then at eighteen, you have no fear! Everything was against me—aircraft inexperience, questionable fuel, and a tight field for takeoff and landing. But I was sure I was up to the challenge, and my guardian angel had automatically been summoned to ride along on this one like the many others to protect me for the plan God had for my life.

The takeoff was normal, but just as we cleared the trees along the road, that big 450 up front let out a horrendous belch and backfired several times as we climbed for altitude. Then it smoothed out, but backfired again at about 1,000 feet. Somehow I was not enjoying this flight! I located the cylinder head temp gage and noticed it was climbing toward the red line. I keyed the intercom and told my buddy that something wasn't right, and I was cutting our flight short to get this bird, and us, back on good ol' terra firma.

Since I wasn't familiar with this military airplane, I decided to make about a three-mile final approach to our forty-acre field. I pulled the sliding canopy back, slowed the airplane down to the approach speed arc marked on the airspeed indicator, and started slowly cranking in some flaps. (The BT-13 had a flap control wheel with a wooden knob located on the left side of the cockpit that manually cranked the wing flaps down.) I knew I had to plant this bird right on the other side of the boundary fence, then stand on the brakes to get it stopped before we went charging through the fence on the other end of the field. We cleared the fence, the wheels touched down in a three point landing (main gear wheels and tailwheel), and I stood on the brakes with the control stick in my lap. We slowed and stopped just short of the fence along the road.

I parked the airplane and shut it down. My first question to my farmer "wannabe" pilot friend was, "Where did you get the aviation fuel? There's something wrong with that fuel to cause the backfiring and the high cylinder head temp."

I could not believe my ears when he replied, "I couldn't get ava gas so I went down to the local Farmer's Exchange *and mixed stove gas half and half with auto gas.*" Wow! What a mixture that was! He thought he could up the octane of auto gas by mixing high octane stove gas with it. No wonder that 450-hp Pratt & Whitney belched as though spitting out a rotten pickle! It was like feeding a connoisseur of gourmet food some gut wrenching slum gullion. Of course my huge mistake was not quizzing him about the fuel *before* the flight rather than *after* the flight. I shudder to think what would have happened if the engine had let out that huge belch just before the trees rather than after we had cleared them. Another lesson learned, and two thumbs up to my guardian angel!

There is a sequel to this story. The next pilot that he got to fly the BT-13 got it out of that tight field okay, but on the landing probably didn't plant it right on the other side of the boundary fence. He apparently touched down with too much speed and went right through the opposite fence bordering the road, wiped off the landing gear when it hit the ditch, skidded across the road on its belly and ended up against the front porch of the farmhouse on the other side. That was the end of that BT-13. What a sad end to a fine airplane! I wish I could have gotten more than twenty minutes flight time in this veteran of World War II.

★ ★ ★ ★ ★ ★ ★ ★ ★ ★ ★ ★ ★

WHO TURNED OUT
THE LIGHTS?

Sometimes doing a favor for a friend can get you in trouble. It was 1947, and the GI Bill Flight Training Program was in full swing. I had gotten a job working in the office of the fixed base operator in Janesville, Wisconsin. My airplane was tied down on the flight line, and by now I had logged some fifty hours in the Stearman. It was an ideal job for a nineteen-year-old. I had become friends with two guys who were learning to fly under the GI Bill. They lived north of Janesville in a lake community.

One evening after a day of flying the Stearman, they asked me if I would fly them home. Their wives had dropped them off earlier in the day, so they were without transportation. I asked if there was an open field that we could land in, and they assured me there was a long field not too far from their homes. Now the Stearman, unlike the Waco UPF-7, has a single seat in the front cockpit. The two of them wedged themselves in the front cockpit, and off we went. It was late afternoon, and I knew the twenty-minute flight would put us there just at dusk. They briefed me on the location of the field that laid east and west near the lake. They said there was a road that bordered the west end of the field. When we arrived over the area, I spotted the field that they were pointing at as we circled overhead. From my experience of flying off hayfields, I knew the cardinal rule was make a low pass across the field to check out the terrain. So I made the low pass from west to east, and in the dim light of dusk, it looked okay. The extra flying around cost me some precious fading daylight time.

Everything was normal as I lined on a final to this make-shift landing field. When you're flying an open cockpit bi-plane from the rear cockpit, you have your head looking forward out the left side of the airplane—you just can't see anything over the nose. Looked like we were on a near perfect approach. Suddenly I felt the airplane lurch, and it looked like a giant Fourth of July sparkler. The sparks started at the left wing N strut and flittered around the front of the airplane to the right side. What was that? My attention was diverted from the approach as I puzzled over what had caused the fireworks!

The next thing I knew, the wheels hit the ground, and we bounced back in the air. I came alive and hit the throttle to ease the airplane down to a flare with power for what I expected would be a normal landing rollout. We touched down alright, but what followed was a wild ride in very rough terrain. It was over the crest of a small hill, then down the other side with me standing on the brakes. Finally, we came to a stop, and at that precise moment there was a bang, and the airplane began shaking violently. I immediately turned the ignition switch off, and the shaking stopped. I scrambled out of the rear cockpit with my two friends right behind me. What I found when I got around to the front of the airplane was a fence post and a shattered wooden propeller—we had run into one lone fence post that had been left in the middle of the field when a fence had been taken down. Just my luck! But what were all those sparks about that we saw on short final? We soon found out. We had hit a power line that lined the western edge of the field running along side the road. For-tunately, as we discovered later, we hit the wires right between two utility poles. There were scorch marks in the paint on the front case of the engine which indicated we had hit the wires straight on. We soon learned that we had put the nearby town of 2,500 completely out of lights. Worse than that, the farmers in the vicinity had been in the middle of milking their cows when their milking machines and barn lights flickered and went out. Oh boy, I'm in BIG trouble now! I couldn't fly the airplane out, and I was afraid the power company would come looking for the guy who severed the power lines.

I had been given a spare wooden prop, but it was back down at the Janesville airport. We drove down to the airport, got the prop, then went back up to the field where the Stearman was sitting. By car headlights we removed the damaged prop and installed the used wooden prop. The plan was to get up at four a.m. and fly the bird out at daybreak. I was hoping I would be long gone by the time anybody came looking for me.

We got out to the airplane just at morning light. For the first time, I got a good look at that field. It was a far cry from what my buddies had described as being a good field! From the road where we hit the power lines the ground went down hill, then there was a slight uphill after which the field became level. However, in addition to the rolling terrain on the western end of the field, there were wires and a utility pole and wires at the eastern end. Beyond that were the lakeshore and cottages scattered along the shore. Not an ideal place to fly out of, to say the least!

My only hope was to get the tail of the airplane back against the fence, hold the brakes to get the engine up to max rpm, then let her go and hope for the best. Since we were on the high side of an incline, I told my two friends to hold against the N struts on each wing, and when I nodded my head, they were to drop to the ground and let the wing pass over them. At full rpm the Stearman was shaking as if to say, "Come on, I'm ready to go." When I was sure I was getting all

I was going to get out of the engine, I nodded my head and released the brakes. It was as though I had been shot out of a sling shot. The airplane accelerated down the hill but lost half of the momentum going up the little hill. When I crested the mound I took a bead on that utility pole down at the other, and I knew I had to clear it or I would end up either in somebody's cottage or in the lake. My short field flying had taught me not to get over anxious and horse the airplane off the ground before you had enough flying speed so it will climb. Otherwise the airplane will get airborne but will be flying in what is called ground effect. So, I held it down, and at the last second, I pulled back on the stick. The Stearman leaped off the ground and cleared the pole—not by much, but enough. The cottages were just beyond, and at fifty feet, I thundered across the roofs of the cottages at five o'clock in the morning. I can see them now—some of the sleeping residents tumbling out of bed wondering what just flew through their bedroom! Out over the lake I breathed a big sigh of relief—relief that I hadn't had to pay for taking down the power lines, and relief that I had made it out of what was the worst hayfield I had ever seen. Oh well, as the saying goes, "All's well that ends well." It was a routine early morning flight back to the Janesville airport, but I was a little early for work.

SOMETHING IN THE AIR
BESIDES FLYING

Who was it that said, "In spring a young man's fancy turns to love"? It happens to all of us, and it happened to me. I was still working in the office at the local flight school when I met a perky, petite, pretty, redheaded cashier. At first I saw her from afar, then talked to her briefly as she waited on me. She had a lovely smile, and that red hair captivated me. Her boss had strategically placed a red spotlight that highlighted her beautiful natural red hair. I was sure she had many guys asking her for dates as she waited on them, so I didn't want to fall into that category of just another one of those guys. If only I could get a proper introduction. I learned that her name was Jo, that was short for Joanne. I knew a cab driver that regularly drove her to work each day, so I asked him to arrange an introduction to this attractive girl who had stirred my romantic instincts. We hatched a plan that would put me in a strategic place where an intro would be casual and appropriate. Whoopee! It worked! Now I could talk to her at work, and if I got real lucky, get a date. It took me a week or so to get my courage up to optimum strength. (Isn't it funny—every guy is afraid to ask fearing a turn down, and every girl is waiting for that certain guy to ask, afraid he won't.) I asked, and she said okay. The evening of our date, she said she wanted me to stop by her house to meet her mother. Oh I see, get Mom's approval up front, huh? Well, that's good, so I put my best foot forward and found her mom to be a very jolly, pleasant person. I also saw where Jo got her red hair. After her mom found out I was a preacher's son, "I was in like Flynn!"

The date went well, although I think I was less of a romantic because of my inexperience. However, other dates followed, and I came up with a few novel ideas to let her know what I was thinking and feeling. Like the time that I bought a little stuffed yellow duck, attached a little note to it and put it on her desk at work. There were other instances where I managed to muster a romantic idea or two, but you have to understand that I had led a sheltered life—sheltered, that is, from everything but flying as the preceding chapters have recounted.

What I lacked in the romantic department I made up for in flying. Soon I was planning a date where I would give her the first airplane ride. The day dawned beautiful, so I picked her up and we drove to the airport. She didn't seem apprehensive as I buckled her in to the front cockpit of my open cockpit biplane. By this time in my flying career, I had introduced number of people to the joys of flight, giving them an easy, pleasant ride. I planned to do the same with Jo, for this was her very first experience to "slip the surly bonds of earth." I made sure I made lazy turns that would not produce the slightest "G" forces on her. This was no time to boast of my prowess as a pilot—I wanted her to be impressed by the fun of flying. We were only up about fifteen minutes when I thought maybe that was enough for her. We couldn't communicate because she was in the front cockpit, and all I could see was the flying helmet she had put on to protect that pretty red hair. So, I came in and landed. When the airplane was just rolling to a stop at mid-runway, she hollered over the idling engine, "We're not quitting already, are we?" Well, that was like saying siccum to a dog! We were still rolling out, so I pushed the throttle full forward and away we went. This time, knowing that she was game for anything, I showed her what flying was all about. Thirty minutes later we landed, and she still had a smile on her face. I found out that she was gung-ho for the wildest carnival rides, some of which *I* wouldn't consider riding! She was eager to tell her friends, most of which had never flown, about her boyfriend giving her a ride in *his* airplane. Score one for Captain Don!

One day we shared a flying experience that I had thought about for a long time. Routinely I had been doing loops, which is a mild aerobatic maneuver but looks and feels spectacular. Normally when you do a loop, you do one and level off. I wanted to see how many consecutive loops I could do without stopping. So on this particular day we climbed up to 5,000 feet, high for us in those days, and began the first loop. When we went over the top and came out at the bottom of the loop, instead of leveling off I pushed the throttle forward and used the extra airspeed to start up into the next loop. I did this one after another, losing a little altitude each time, but succeeding to break my own record of only one loop at a time. By the time we had done nine or ten consecutive loops my right arm was getting so weak from pulling back on the control stick that I now was using both hands to pull it up and around. Not a record I'm sure, but it sure was a lot of fun. And Jo? She thought it beat any carnival ride she had ever been on!

This is not a romance novel, so I will spare you all the details of the ups and downs of our courtship and engagement. I will gladly tell you that Jo and I were married on June 18th, 1949, in her family's church, the Evangelical United Brethren Church in Janesville, Wisconsin. This began a life commitment to each other which produced two daughters, Nancy Jo and Linda Sue. God had some work and polishing to do in our lives, but in His own timing it led to a lifetime of committed service to our Lord. Succeeding chapters will reveal how God used the training and flying experiences of my youth in His service.

BARN YARD LANDING

I had put about 100 flight hours on the Stearman and thoroughly enjoyed every hour. One day while I was working in the flight school office, a Waco UPF-7 landed and taxied up near the office. It was a sharp-looking airplane with its red and white paint job and sunburst striping on the top of the wing panels. When the pilot walked into the office, he asked who owned the Stearman, and I confessed that it was mine. I wasn't prepared for his next question: "How would you like to trade airplanes?" Well, I hadn't considered selling or trading the Stearman when I came to work that day, but it was an intriguing thought. We walked out to look over each other's airplanes. The UPF-7 had the same Continental 220-hp engine as the Stearman. In fact, both airplanes were much alike as they were used as primary trainers during World War II. Many of the fighter and bomber pilots of Second World War learned to fly in these airplanes. I knew my Stearman would soon need the rib stitching replaced on the top wings, so the thought of trading presented a convenient way out of a lot of work. The big attraction to me, though, was the larger front cockpit of the Waco that was designed to seat two people side by side. It also had dual controls for giving flight instruction. So, we agreed to swap airplanes, no money involved, and exchanged bills of sale on the spot. I admit I had a twinge of sadness as I watched my Stearman takeoff and disappear into the distance without me. We had shared some interesting experiences, my Stearman and I.

The UPF-7 performed about the same as the Stearman, and I enjoyed being able to give rides two passengers at a time. One nice thing about the Waco, unlike the Stearman, was that it had a wide landing gear. You would have to be a very poor pilot to get it to ground loop. In the little over a year that I kept the Waco, my flying had been enjoyable but very routine . . . until one day!

I had flown down to my hometown, Warren, Illinois, to see my parents and my little sister. I spent the day with them, then cranked up and headed back to Janesville. I had made one circle around my girlfriend Jo's house, then entered the traffic pattern at the airport. I was on the downwind leg to runway twenty-two when the engine began to sputter and died! I immediately reached down to the fuel selector to switch to the other wing tank. The engine roared back to life, and I turned on to the base leg of the rectangular traffic pattern. But the power was short lived and quit again. I was out of fuel! This is the unpardonable sin for any pilot, but you have to know how I managed to fly on a low budget those days. Knowing the approximate fuel consumption per hour, I had it figured that I could fly forty-five minutes on $3.00 worth of fuel. Of course, I had doubled that for my sixty minute round trip flight to Warren, so I should have had about thirty minutes of fuel left when I got back to the airport. Wrong! I was plumb out of fuel in the airport traffic pattern! When the engine quit the second time I immediately rolled into a left bank hoping I could make the runway.

There was a strong southwest wind that day and as soon I was headed into the wind my forward speed over the ground slowed by twenty or twenty-five mph. Then, to further complicate my situation, lining the perimeter of the airport boundary was a row of very tall cottonwood trees. Just beyond the trees and to the right was a farm barnyard. I saw that it was closer than the runway, so I opted to head for it hoping that I could plant the airplane in the barnyard, in one piece, that is. There is a saying among pilots that if an airplane has crashed that he "bought the farm." I was hoping for better. My only chance to clear those cottonwood trees was to nose the airplane down, pick up some much needed airspeed, then haul back on the stick to hopefully soar over the trees. It worked! I made it over the trees alright, but my airspeed dissipated and the airplane stalled at about fifty feet and mushed down to a very hard kerplunk in the middle of the barnyard. I was sure that the landing gear must be broken, but as I climbed out, I was surprised to see that it was still intact. Fortunately, there were no cows in the barnyard, so I hopped over the fence and walked to the hangar to get some fuel.

The guys that were standing around looked at me, then out to the flight line, then back at me and said, *"Where's your airplane?"*

"Over there in the barnyard," I pointed.

I got a five gallon can of fuel and carried it over the barnyard fence to the airplane. With some fuel now sloshing in the bottom of the tank, the engine came to life again. I did a short field takeoff, cleared the four foot fence and landed inside the airport. But my airplane presence back on the flight line was wafting a peculiar smell, and some of the guys were holding their noses! After that takeoff run in the barnyard, my airplane looked like a manure spreader and smelled like one too! Chalk one up to experience, Don, and give your overworked guardian angel a friendly nod.

'ROUND AND 'ROUND
WE GO

It was a beautiful Sunday afternoon when, after church and dinner, Jo and I pulled into the airport parking lot where I parked my airplane. We were surprised to see our neighbors sitting in their car as though waiting for us to arrive. I had told my neighbor that sometime I would give him an airplane ride, and I guess he thought this might be his lucky day.

Before our wedding, I had sold my Waco UPF-7—I didn't think I could support two loves. But nearly a year later, I had been convinced by a pilot friend that he had just the airplane for me—an Aeronca Low Wing. What was that?! It was a two place airplane with a ninety-hp five-cylinder radial engine up front. I learned later that the reason he was willing to sell it to me for $450 was that it had scared him so badly the first time he flew it that after he landed, he said he would never get in that airplane again! I should have gotten a clue when on the appointed day he got a flight instructor to give me a demo ride in N15292. As far as I could tell from the passenger seat it flew like any other airplane, so I bought it. It was not at all like the popular Aeronca Champ or Aeronca Chief airplanes. It was faster, had a higher stall speed, and required a higher climb out and approach airspeed, or things could get very hairy. Anything below eighty mph indicated airspeed and the airplane became very unstable. In fact, that airplane had a slight tail flutter when the airspeed got below eighty mph. I found that out on the second flight after I bought it, when I took it up to do some stalls to see if the airplane had any bad characteristics. It stalled pretty clean, but when I recovered, if I leveled off below eighty, the tail would oscillate up and down as though you were riding over a series of gentle speed bumps. The first time I noticed it, I pressed my face against the side glass and I could see the tip of the horizontal stabilizer going up and down. It flew perfectly otherwise.

So we greeted our neighbors, and I prepared to give him a ride. The Aeronca was tied down in front of a T-hangar with another row of airplanes parked in front. The airplanes on both sides of mine were out flying, as was the airplane directly in front of the Aeronca. Those were the days when most small airplanes didn't have starters, and you swung the prop to start the engine. I put my passenger in the airplane and showed him where the throttle and the mag (ignition) switch was located. It was a risky practice, but I had done this many, many times when giving rides and no experienced guy was around to "give me a prop." So I briefed him on the procedure. This particular engine had a primer system on the carburetor which worked when you pumped the throttle in and out. I told him that when I said, "Contact" or "Switch On" he was to pull the throttle back and turn on the mag switch. As a precaution, I left tie-down ropes tied to both wings and the tail.

Our wives were watching from a short distance away. I started pulling the prop through as my passenger pumped the throttle. I then called for "Switch On," and he responded with "Okay." A flick of the prop, and the engine started. I began to walk around the right wing when I was suddenly aware that the engine wasn't idling but was winding up to a full roar! Just as I got to the right wing tip, the straining airplane broke the rope tied to the tail. In rapid succession, the rope on the left wing broke as the airplane strained forward, and then the rope on the right wing broke. This all happened in a matter of seconds. When the last rope broke, I was just going around the right wing tip. I immediately grabbed the hand hold in the wing tip. Here I am in my Sunday go-to-meeting duds desperately trying to keep the airplane from crashing into other airplanes parked nearby, or worst case scenario, taking off without me. All I could do was to dig my heels into the turf and hang on! Our wives looked on in utter amazement as I kept the airplane going in circles like a boy with a wire-controlled model airplane. I was frantically signaling him to pull back on the throttle. (He had failed to pull the throttle back during our pre-start procedure, so it was revving up to takeoff rpm!) I will never forget the frantic look on his face as he looked out the side window at me with eyes as big as saucers, then took both fists and pounded on the instrument panel. By this time I was getting winded, and we had already made several circles in that tight open area with other airplanes parked nearby. I finally used a finger across the throat to get him to cut the mag switch. Finally, finally, remembering my first "pull back" signal, he pulled the throttle back, the engine wound down to idle, the airplane came to a stop, and I let go of the grip I had on the wing tip. Other than the grass stains on the cuffs of my gabardine wedding suit and dirty dress shoes, I was okay, although a little winded.

Surely this had already been a wild first airplane ride that could never compare with anything in an actual flight. I had expected him to come scrambling out the cabin door and head on a dead run for the parking lot. But he stayed in his seat and indicated he still wanted to go for it. So, I climbed in, closed the door, waved to our stunned wives, pushed the throttle full forward, and took off. Somehow, I still doubt that he *really* enjoyed the flight. I know I shall never forget the day I kept an airplane going in circles like a cowboy with a stallion on a rope at full gallop!

Aeronca NI5292 and I had many good hours together, and I hated to see her go. But the Lord was spiritually tapping me on the shoulder to get my attention about serving Him. My Christian life had been in a holding pattern, and I knew it was time to give Him the controls of my life. Certainly He had been my unseen copilot through many flight experiences, some of which I have recounted in these pages. His hand on my life had to be for a higher purpose, so I yielded to His sovereign plan, and my life has never been the same.

An interesting aside to this story is that fifty years later I located my old airplane. Aeronca Low Wing NI5292 now proudly resides in the EAA (Experimental Aircraft Association) museum in Lakeland, Florida. It had been restored to mint condition and donated to the EAA to preserve one of the last, if not *the* last, Aeronca Low Wing left flying. When I owned it in 1950, there were only about fifteen left on the FAA registry. I have visited her several times during the past few years, and each visit rekindles some thoughts of our flights together, including the one in this chapter.

FLYING THE BAMBOO BOMBER

Two years after I had dedicated my life to the Lord and one year after my wife Jo accepted Christ as her Savior, we were on our way to Bob Jones University in Greenville, South Carolina. It was a big step of faith for us that not all of our family fully approved, but we were committed to following the Lord wherever He led. We choose BJU because both of us had been challenged spiritually by a summer evangelistic team from the school.

That fall I became acquainted with a group of men who had launched a fledging mission named Globe Missions. They had purchased a twin engine Cessna T-50 and were looking for someone to fly it and become the mission pilot. By this time I had something over 300 hours, but I had never flown a twin engine airplane! I always have felt that basically all airplanes fly the same—only the performance numbers (stall, climb, approach speeds) are different. So I was eager to get acquainted with this twin engine bird.

I took the flight manual home and studied it from cover to cover. The Cessna AT-50 was the military version of the civilian UC-78 model. The AT-50 was dubbed the Bamboo Bomber because of its wood and fabric construction. It was used as an advanced trainer during WWII, along with the Beech AT-11, to train bomber pilots. The Cessna had two

Jacobs 225 hp radial engines with non-feathering props. (This airplane wouldn't maintain altitude on one engine because of a wind milling prop that couldn't be feathered.) The cabin was configured with pilot and copilot seats up front, and a bench seat for three passengers in back. I remembered the Cessna UC-78 that was based at the Janesville, Wisconsin, airport. It was owned and operated by the Janesville Parker Pen Company as their executive airplane before the war. As a young pilot, I was in awe of that airplane and the pilot who flew it.

So, I sat in the cockpit of the Cessna for thirty minutes getting acquainted with where everything was located on the instrument panel and in the cockpit. I had learned the starting sequence from the flight manual, so I cranked up the engines and spent fifteen minutes taxiing it around. Finally I bit the bullet and took off. I retracted the landing gear and flew it around for an hour just getting the feel of the airplane. The landing was uneventful, meaning I didn't bounce it and I kept it going straight down the runway centerline.

You have to understand that this was 1951 and flying a twin engine airplane without an official checkout wasn't all that unusual for those of us who cut our teeth on hayfield-type flying. After I soloed the Cub, I never was checked out by another pilot in any of the airplanes that I flew—the Stearman PT-17, the Vultee BT-13, and others. I was a confident young man and very much at home in any airplane. It would be a number of years before I got my multi-engine rating put on my pilot certificate.

One incident with the T-50 tested my pilot abilities to the max. I had flown the Globe Missions executives from Greenville to Bristol, Tennessee, on the other side of the Blue Ridge Mountains. The day we planned to depart Bristol dawned with smoke from a forest fire blanketing the area. I had started the engines a couple of times to move the airplane, which drained the batteries. I felt sure once airborne and heading south we would soon fly out of the smoky area. So I loaded the passengers, taxied out to the runway, did the run up and started the takeoff. As soon as we lifted off, I hit the gear up switch to retract the landing gear. It was an electrically operated gear retraction system. I could hear the electric motor located under my seat humming as it pulled the gear up. But then it stopped. Too soon, I thought, as I looked at the landing gear instrument on the panel. It showed the wheels about half way to the up position. Obviously the gear motor had drained the last juice out of the batteries, and the generators hadn't run long enough to recharge them. For every aircraft system there is a backup, and the backup on this airplane was a crank stowed under the pilot's seat which allowed the pilot or copilot to manually crank the landing gear down, in this case fully down.

We had flown the runway heading beyond the point where you normally would make a left turn and depart on course, so the airport was well behind us. By this time I had decided that the smoke so restricted the forward visibility that I wanted to get this bird back on the ground. Two left turns to the downwind leg, but the airport that should have been on our left wasn't where it was supposed to be. It was totally obscured by the heavy blanket of smoke. Navigational systems were still in the future for most of us, so I resorted to the way we always navigated on cross country flights, by landmarks. I spotted the two-lane highway that we had traveled to the airport, and knowing that it would lead us to the airport, I followed it and made all the turns the road made. Sure enough, the airport suddenly appeared as a phantom out of the smoke. I circled across mid-field and lined up on a short final to a normal landing. But when I hit the switch to lower the landing gear, I heard the motor start, and before the green gear down light came on the instrument panel, the motor stopped. At the same time, there was no electrical power to any of the other instruments. We had drained the battery.

The generators had not had a chance to recharge it after starting the engines several times. But there was an emergency method to lower the landing gear. Insert the crank and start cranking it down. While I flew the airplane and kept the airport in sight, the man sitting in the copilot seat got the job. He was still cranking as I was on final to the runway. We landed without further incident. The mission leaders went home by car, and I stood by waiting for VFR (Visual Flight Rules) weather. Two days later the wind had switched and the skies returned to blue, and I took off for my flight back to Greenville.

My association with Globe Missions was a prelude to mission flying, but the Lord had some preparation and polishing to do in my life before He could use me in missionary aviation. I thought I was ready, but He knew I was not. At that point in my life I had acquired a habit—like a drug addict, I was addicted to flying! I really was looking for a way to support "my habit." Oh, I wanted to serve the Lord all right, but on my terms. I had not yet come to the place where I was willing to surrender my will to His. In my mind it was a foregone conclusion that I would fly airplanes for Him. I was still telling the Lord how I would serve Him, rather than He telling me how He wanted me to serve. That spiritual battle came later, but it didn't come easy. I struggled for six months before I could honestly say, *"Lord, if I never fly again it's okay."* I had said it many times before in prayer, but getting up off my knees I knew it wasn't true. How could I possibly give up my love for flying? But one day I knew it was true—God had won the battle of wills when I surrendered. I laid my love for flying on the altar of sacrifice, and now I waited on Him to show me where and how He wanted me to serve Him. My "addiction" no longer had a hold on me.

The validity of my decision was confirmed when I could drive past an airport and resist the uncontrollable urge to turn in and browse around the airplanes. It took my dear wife Jo another six months before she believed it, because too many times I had lingered and the dinner she had faithfully prepared was spoiled because I was at the airport. Even a legitimate delay would be met with a *"I know where you were! You were out at the airport."* The truth of my commitment was further proven by a span of nearly eight years when the Lord led me into youth evangelism with Youth for Christ, and I only flew enough to keep current.

It is so much like our Heavenly Father to, once we have given Him our most precious possession, lovingly give it back. The succeeding chapters demonstrate the depth of God's love in giving His children the *"desires of your heart."*

BANNER TOWING

In 1953, I had taken a job as a spot announcement writer and a special events reporter with a radio station in Bristol, Tennessee. Bristol was the home town of Tennessee Ernie Ford, and the station were I worked was where he got his start in radio. From there he went on to national acclaim as a recording artist and TV personality. This was also the town where our youngest daughter Linda was born.

Early on, I had checked out the small airport at the edge of town, and soon was able to do some part time flying towing banners for the local FBO (Fixed Base Operator). It was interesting flying. He had an eighty-five hp Piper Cub that on a good day could snatch a banner with five foot high letters into the air. Sometimes it was a little hairy! Like the day I had twenty-six letters laid out at a forty-five degree angle down the runway with the rope attached to the Cub's tow hook. The trick was to hold the brakes, get the engine revving up to max rpm so that all eighty-five horses were at full gallop, then release the brakes and after a short run pull the airplane up in a steep climb while looking back out the open side watching for the first letter to peal off the ground. As I remember, we had a 450-foot rope between the first letter of the banner and the tail of the airplane. By having the banner laid out down the runway, you had 900 feet before the first letter started to peal up. By then you wanted to have climbed to 100 feet, then level off as the rest of the banner became airborne. That was a hot summer day which didn't make for max aircraft performance. I watched as the first letter came off, then each of the other letters came up *except* the last letter. It was dragging along down the sod runway flat on the ground, catching on tuffs of grass as it went. Every time it caught on a clump of grass it felt like some cowboy had lassoed the tail of the airplane! It seemed like the Cub, with engine putting out all eighty-five horses, stopped momentarily and each time lost about twenty-five feet of altitude. With the end of the runway coming up rapidly it was time to cut the banner loose before the airplane stalled. I pulled the release cable, and it felt like somebody had given me a boot in the posterior. It was almost like that Cub was saying, "Thank goodness!" I came around, landed, and repositioned the banner for another try. That day I tried twice more to get that banner up, and on the third try the banner came up and sashayed through the bushes until that old Cub clawed its way up to 500, then 1,000 feet. Of course, that twenty-six letter banner was too long for an eighty-five hp Cub, and we never tried that many letters again.

In 1954, I learned of an organization called Youth for Christ International that was holding their first YFC Director's School in Kansas City. It was during those days that we were prayerfully seeking God's will for our lives. This would put our faith to the test since I would have to resign my position at the radio station in order to attend the two-week training school. So, after much prayer, Jo and I made the decision for me to enroll. YFCI was recruiting directors for YFC programs being established all across the U.S. Following school completion and interviews, they would recommend graduates to cities seeking a YFC Director for a youth evangelism outreach.

So, I resigned my job at the radio station, we packed up our meager belongings, loaded four-year-old Nancy and infant Linda in our 1948 Chrysler, and headed out of Bristol on our way to a still uncertain future. Jo and our girls stayed with her folks in Wisconsin while I headed for Kansas City.

After graduation from the intensive two-week YFC Director's Training School, we were sent to South Bend, Indiana, for an interview with the Board of St. Joseph County Youth for Christ. Their program was already in full swing, with biweekly YFC Rallies on Saturday night, and YFC Bible Clubs in all of the county high schools. These were big shoes to fill, and I spent many midnight hours catching up to the pace the former director had set.

Following a successful two years in South Bend, I was called to step up to the position of Area VP of YFCI in eastern Canada. The office was located in Toronto, and my job as was to oversee and assist the YFC program in Ontario province and elsewhere in eastern Canada. I found myself once again stepping into big shoes, this time of the former Canadian director who had moved up to a position in the YFC International office in Wheaton, Illinois.

Six months into my administration, I was approached by Paul Hartford, the area vice president for YFCI in the Caribbean. He had heard that I was a licensed pilot with several years flight experience, and he challenged me to join him in developing YFC in the islands. He was a highly experienced pilot who had pioneered missionary aviation in the forties. He was flying a twin engine Piper Apache to cover the islands from the Bahamas to Trinidad. It was almost too good to be true—an opportunity to realize my initial call to missionary aviation! But there were many challenges to be met before this became a reality and the fulfillment of a "call" of God.

EMERGENCY CRASH LANDING

In the early days of our Youth for Christ ministry in the Bahamas, I was using a Piper Tri Pacer, sometimes known among pilots as a "Fly Paster," to get our YFC program off and running. I had a coworker who flew with me on our weekend YFC itinerary to the islands. We played the trumpet and led the singing. Special music was an instrumental duet—it was an accordion and trumpet combo. We had held our Friday night youth rally at Marsh Harbor on the island of Abaco, and on Saturday morning we took off for our next stop at the island of Spanish Wells. The weather was deteriorating, but I decided to make a run for it since the young people looked forward to our coming. We flew under the overcast, but halfway to our destination we ran into a squall line and had to do a 180 back to Marsh Harbor.

While having dinner, we heard a Florida radio station announce that the hurricane that had been churning up the water south of Havana, Cuba, had turned and was forecast to hit South Florida. This was disturbing news. Both my coworker and I had a wife and children back in West Palm Beach that could be in harm's way. We needed to be there with them if that hurricane came north from Miami as it was forecast. We decided to fly back to Florida ASAP, but we needed to replace the fuel we had burned trying to get to our next YFC rally stop. The Marsh Harbor airstrip had no aviation fuel, but we found a man who had some aviation fuel in a 55 gallon drum. We got 15 gallons, put it in the empty wing tank, and departed for the 200 mile flight back to Florida and home.

It was a rough ride as we fought the feederband winds of the hurricane. Because of the rain squalls we were encountering, we had to deviate from our normal direct course for West Palm Beach. We made the Florida shoreline and turned north to fly up to WPB. I had to switch to the tank with the questionable fuel. As we approached PBIA, there was a large rain squall right over the airport. I turned west thinking I could come in behind the rain for a landing at the airport when it happened! Just as I turned to westward heading, the engine began to sputter and then it quit! At only 600 feet, I knew that I had less than a minute before we would be on the ground somewhere! Since I was downwind, I instinctively made an immediate 180 to get into the wind which would slow down the landing speed. I looked vainly for a cleared field, but all I saw was trees and some houses along a canal. One open area was dead ahead—it was the back yard of one of the houses! Hardly a suitable landing field, but it was all I had! We cleared the trees but crunched down to a very hard landing in that back yard right along the canal. Without a shoulder harness, my head went into the instrument panel. When I straightened up, blood was dripping on the front of my white shirt from a gash in my forehead. To my left I saw the landing gear wheel spinning next to my window—yep, we had made a *hard* landing alright! Looking to my right, I saw my passenger hanging half way out of the open cabin door, swaying back and worth moaning as he hung by his seat belt. I knew we needed to get out, so I reached over, unbuckled his belt and urged him to get out. Gradually he began to move, but because the right wing was out over the canal, we had to exit on our hands and knees. I was right behind him, and when I saw him stand up I thought, *Praise the Lord, he's okay.* But he wasn't! He was walking in circles holding his back say, "Oh my back," over and over. Then he asked me, "Does anybody know what happened?" I explained that we had a hard emergency landing. He would acknowledge that information, but repeat his question again. I decided we had better get some help. I walked up to the back door of the house and knocked. No answer, so I knocked again and again. *No one was home!*

I went back to survey the damage. Both landing gears were broken, and the airplane was resting on its belly. Otherwise it was all intact. Just then a swamp buggy appeared on the other side of the canal. He had heard us go over his house, heard the engine die, and came looking for us to see if he could help. I told him we needed help to get to the hospital if he could get to our side of the canal. He did and took us to the local hospital.

The emergency room doctor was stitching the gash in my forehead, while a nurse was getting some info from my buddy. She came over to the doctor and asked him if he had ever heard of the doctor that my friend had given in response to her question. The doctor said no. We found out later that he had given the name of a doctor in Grand Rapids, Michigan, when he was a boy. It was then that they realized that he had a mild concussion. They kept him for a few days until his memory returned. Me? Well, I didn't let on, but my back was killing me! I didn't want them to hospitalize me, too, and incur that extra expense.

So, I changed my clothes at the hospital, got in my car and drove home. What a shock it was for my poor wife Jo when I walked in with a big bandage across my forehead! I laid on a heating pad for two weeks before I could walk normally. To this day I have trouble with my lower back.

Would you say that my guardian angel was on the job big time that day?

BABY IN A SHOE BOX

Years later, the silence of the night hours was suddenly broken and I was jarred awake by the incessant ringing of my bedside telephone. It was 5 o'clock in the morning, and this usually means something has happened to family member or friend.

I picked up the phone and heard a voice identify himself and say, "Don, we have a new baby girl."

And I thought, *Why is this missionary calling me at this hour to announce a new baby?*

Then the caller continued saying, "But she is premature and is turning blue. The government nurse said we must get her to a hospital right away. Can you come?"

By this time I was wide awake, and I said, "I'll be in the air as soon as I can get to the airport."

I hurriedly got dressed and briefed my wife on what was happening. I told her to call the hospital that was just across from the airport in Florida and have them on stand-by for a preemie that was being flown in from the islands. We lived less than a mile from the airport where I kept the airplane, and after a *very* brief preflight I was taxing out to the runway for takeoff. My faithful Twin Navion was climbing eastward out over the gulf stream of the Atlantic as the darkness gave way to the rising sun. A multitude of thoughts crowded my mind—Would I be in time to save this fragile little life?—Would my wife Jo be able to get everybody alerted to this emergency?—And would the hospital staff be ready? I breathed a prayer to my omni-present "copilot" as I leveled off at 2,500 feet. The 200 mile flight to the island in the Bahamas where this missionary couple served normally took about an hour and a half. But if I whipped the horses in those two engines a little, I could probably shave ten minutes off that flight time. So, with the throttles firewalled, the two "horses" were at full gallop.

I strained my eyes for the contour of Abaco Island, and as it came into view, I could see the airstrip runway dead ahead. A straight in final approach and I was rolling out toward a small group of people waiting for my arrival. I handed my arrival and departure papers to the customs and immigration officer and prepared for a quick turn around. Another missionary wife was holding the tiny bundle, and I learned she was going along to hold the baby. Good idea—how do you fly an airplane and hold a baby too?! A hurried goodbye, a promise of their prayers, and we were rolling for takeoff. I couldn't help being concerned wondering how my smallest passenger was doing. A silent prayer for the Lord to hold this little life in his hand, and soon the shore line of Florida was on the horizon .

By radio I had advised U.S. Customs and Immigration of our emergency flight and obtained permission to bypass normal U.S. clearance procedure, and fly directly to the smaller airport next to the hospital. I would take care of proper clearance later after the emergency was over. I also asked Palm Beach Approach Control to call my wife and alert her to our present position and our landing ETA. To save time, I opted to make a straight in approach to runway twenty-seven. The location of our house was just north of the flight path of runways nine and twenty-seven. Over the years I had used the changing of the pitch of the props as a signal to my wife Jo of my arrival home, and I did it as I was abreast of my house just off my right wing. I learned later that at that moment Jo had the hospital on the telephone and was able to advise them that the flight with the premature baby was landing.

Since my car was parked at the airport, and the hospital was across from the west side of the airport, there was no need for an ambulance. Ten minutes after landing and shutting down, we were at the hospital emergency room doors. The doors opened, and just inside stood hospital personnel waiting for our arrival. They took the baby and immediately began checking her vital signs. Of course we were not allowed in the emergency room, but soon a nurse came out to tell us this little girl was safely in an hospital incubator and all of our efforts had paid off—she had a good chance of making it through the next critical hours. It was then that she told us that the baby weighed an astounding two pounds eleven ounces! We caught a glimpse of her in the incubator as they took her up to the critical care nursery. I could not believe what a tiny, tiny baby I was seeing. The bundle of blankets had looked rather large on the flight over, but she was oh, so tiny. I found out later that the baby's first crib was a shoe box! Yes, a shoe box!

I cannot express the feeling of quiet satisfaction that flooded over me as I was leaving the hospital knowing that God had allowed Jo and me to lend a helping hand to a missionary couple in their time of need and be God's instrument in saving this tiny life. Yes, she did survive and I had the privilege of flying her and her parents back to their mission station two months later. Praise the Lord!

MEN THAT IMPACTED MY LIFE

My life has been impacted by three Godly men: my preacher father, missionary Don Moffat, and missionary aviation pioneer Paul C. Hartford.

My dear dad set the example for me of a Godly man and faithful preacher of God's Word. I spent many hours with him in his study as a boy, and he taught me things that I remember and practice to this day. I dearly loved my dad, and though he has been with the Lord many years now, I still miss him.

I was sixteen and was learning to fly as described in earlier chapters. Dad asked me to go with him to a pastor's conference, and I jumped at the chance to be with him one on one. Little did I know how that trip would change the course of my life! A featured speaker was missionary Don Moffat, who had just returned from the mission field in South America. As most sixteen-year-olds, I was a little bored with the whole thing and probably showed it as I sat slumped down in my seat. I shall never forget the first sentence that he uttered to that conclave of preachers. *"Brethren, we MUST employ the use of the airplane to get the missionary out of the boat and off the mule."* When he said that magic word *airplane*, I came alive. Needless to say, that got my full attention! Sitting bolt upright in my seat, I listened intently as he went on to describe how hours and sometime days were being spent by missionaries just getting to remote villages deep in the jungle to share the Gospel. A small plane could make the same trip in minutes instead of hours, speeding the advance of the gospel to the unreached tribes. Already this concept was being advanced by a pioneer preacher/pilot Paul Hartford, who had this vision and had proved the validity of what Don Moffat was saying.

That day marked the beginning of what was to be my "call" to missionary aviation. I did not realize it then, because I was still focused on pursuing a career in commercial aviation as an airline pilot. But the seed that was sown in that encounter was to be further nurtured by subsequent encounters and events that kept me pointed in the direction that God had ordained. I never got away from that missionary's cry for help: *"Let's get the missionary out of the boat and off the mule!"* The airplane is the key tool to speed the "good news" of salvation to the lost in hard-to-reach places in the world.

My dear dad was deeply concerned about his sixteen-year-old son, and he had a right to be. Sometime after that pastor's conference he heard that missionary pilot Paul Hartford was going to be at the YFC (Youth for Christ) rally at Freeport, Illinois—a town near by. He was pretty sure I would like to go, given the fact that Hartford was a pilot, so he mentioned it to me. I was, and we went. Paul Hartford had flown in to Hillcrest Airport at Freeport in his Fairchild 24. He played the cornet and gave a stirring challenge to the assembled young people and adults. After closing prayer, I made a beeline for the platform. I wanted to meet this man who for me personified missionary aviation. I had a brief conversation with him, and I managed to inform him of where I was in my flight training. He invited me to come to Winona Lake, Indiana, where he had set up the first Missionary Aviation Flight Training School. Score one for another encounter to nurture the seed of missionary aviation service that had been sown in my heart months before.

That next summer I decided to go the Winona Lake, Indiana, and see Paul and his school. He had purchased a farm north of town that had a north/south grass runway, a couple of hangars, and three Aeronca trainers. It was a good start to specialized flight training for missionary pilots which was later picked up by several Christian institutions as a part of their academic curriculum. Paul Hartford was a true pioneer in the field of missionary aviation. Not only had Paul Hartford championed the use of the small-single engine aircraft on the mission field, but he organized the first conference of Christian airmen which later became a world-wide service serving missions with the light airplane. Little did I know that my premature visit to his fledging missionary pilot training school at Winona Lake would in a few short years find me working and flying with him in Youth for Christ, where he was YFCI area vice president for the Caribbean islands.

GETTING FLIGHT EXPERIENCE THE HARD WAY!

The Beech Model 18 is a really good airplane! I loved flying it. This twin engine bird carried eight passengers and had a rugged airframe for which I shall always thank Walter Beech!

MFI had just purchased the first Twin Beech as a step up to a larger, more capable missionary airplane. I hadn't yet had a check-out in the airplane because we were occupied in getting it ready for missionary service. One day I overheard the owner of the flight service where we were refurbishing our airplane ask a free lance pilot if he would go down to Miami and fly a Twin Beech back to Ft. Lauderdale. I immediately thought this was a great opportunity for me to get some right seat experience in preparation to my upcoming check-out in the airplane. Little did I know how much experience I would get that day!

After lunch we flew down to Miami International Airport to get the Twin Beech. We did the usual preflight inspection, fired up the two Pratt & Whitney radial engines, and taxied to the active runway. As the pilot-in-command was going through the run-up procedure, I noticed he flipped the safety guard off two toggle switches at the base of the throttle pedestal, moved the switches down and returned them to the center position. The tower cleared us for takeoff on nine left, and we were rolling for takeoff. I was completely absorbed by everything that was going on in the cockpit, mentally recording it all for future reference.

The first hint of trouble was when the captain pulled the gear retract handle and it wouldn't budge. He tried several times as we climbed out, and then I heard the tower advise us that *"Your gear is still down."* The captain had just advised the tower we were coming back to land when the right engine started to lose power. I watched him adjusting the throttle on that engine, but it was still losing power. He was just reaching for the prop-feathering button, the first step in shutting down an engine in flight, when the left engine also began winding down. Now both engines were slowing to a complete stop, and we were only 600 feet in the air! I shall never forget the ensuing moments. Not a word was spoken in the cockpit. I felt a sickening knot tightening up right in the center of my solar plexus. We were in trouble! We had turned from our easterly heading to a westbound downwind to land when the engines quit. Realizing there was an emergency in the making, the Miami Tower began clearing all airline traffic out of the landing pattern. The runway was ours—that is, if we could make it!

As the pilot made an immediate left turn toward the runway, it was very evident that we were not going to find refuge in the safety of that beckoning strip of concrete. The first thing I saw in the windshield as we made like a glider was a parking lot full of cars. I knew landing on top of those cars would be disastrous. But then he made another slight turn to the left, and I saw a large drainage canal dead ahead. I remember thinking, *Oh, no, we'll have to swim out of this thing.*

Another slight left turn headed us toward the northwest airport boundary, but outside the fence! Everything went into fast forward from that point. Our right main gear wheel touched down just two feet on the other side of that canal (I later went over to the canal and saw the wheel mark on the end of the bank), rolled across the two lane perimeter road at a forty-five degree angle, and at eighty mph we went through the six-foot chain link fence that surrounded Miami International Airport like it was butter. But the landing roll was far from over! A double utility pole loomed larger than life in front of us, and the pilot deftly maneuvered our stricken aircraft between the double poles and steel guy wires. We came through okay, but we left six feet of the left wing and about eight feet of the right wing behind! He then avoided slamming into a drainage ditch by a slight right turn, and that's when I saw it–that chain link fence again! I thought, *Not the fence again!* and slid my toes up on the top of the rudder pedals to apply the brakes. I don't know if it was me or him, but we got braking action and stopped fifty feet short of the fence.

Instinct tells you to get out, and my reflexes were especially good that day. My "six-foot-four" beat his "five-foot-ten" out of the cockpit and out the cabin door! We ran off about fifty feet, and when we turned to look at the airplane, the sight was right out of a comic movie. There she sat, a crippled bird with torn wings, looking even more forlorn with 100 feet of that chain link fence draped around the nose and wing stubs with ten two-inch steel posts still attached!

The wail of the sirens from the crash trucks was fast approaching. It was then that the pilot walked back to the airplane, went inside, then came out. The crash trucks arrived, and since there was no fire or injuries, asked some questions and left. My associate who had flown us down in a Cessna 172 had followed our takeoff, and when we reported mechanical trouble, the tower vectored him out of the traffic pattern. He finally was able to land and belatedly came up just after the crash vehicles had gone. He was as white as a ghost, but relieved when he saw that we were on our feet and obviously uninjured. The three of us walked over to the airplane, and I pulled on the left engine prop. It wouldn't budge. The engine had ceased and wouldn't turn even when I hung all my weight on the prop.

After filing a report with the FAA, we were ready to fly the Cessna 172 back to Ft. Lauderdale. As my associate and I walked up to the Cessna, I had opened the passenger door on the right side since he was the pilot. He opened his left side door and just stood there. Then he said, "I can't fly this home . . . can you?" He was obviously very shook up. I said, "Sure, I'll fly," and climbed in to the left seat.

Now, unknown to me, my wife and two daughters had received a call from a friend who had heard about a Twin Beech that had just crashed at Miami International Airport. It was on the six o'clock evening news, and they also gave the name of the occupants of the airplane. So our church friend called my wife and said "Jo, can I help you in any way?" Jo asked why, and he then told her about the news he had just heard on the Miami radio station. Frankly, I had already decided that I wouldn't tell her what had happened because it would cause her to worry, especially since our double engine failure was on the same type of aircraft that we were preparing as an upgrade for MFI. Because I was going to be delayed, I had called home and told my girls that I would be a little late, but I'd be home soon.

When I drove in our driveway after I had flown the Twin Navion up from Ft. Lauderdale, there stood Jo and my two girls. I got out and Nancy and Linda ran up saying, "Daddy, are you alright?" Then I heard how they had received the phone call.

We later determined that the cause of both engines failing was that there was no oil in the engines. What had happened was that this pilot had inadvertently closed off the electrically operated oil supply switches when he reached down at the bottom of the throttle pedestal and pulled the switches up. That closed the valve from the oil tank to the engines. I learned that just returning those toggle switched to the neutral position would not open the valve again—it would have had to be moved to the opposite position, then back to neutral. So, there had been just enough oil in the engines to get us to the runway, do the run-up and takeoff before the engine bearings ceased.

I had gone only to get a little first-hand experience in a Twin Beech. What I got was a whole lot of experience but not the kind I was expecting. Another thumbs up to my overworked guardian angel!

THE DESIRES OF YOUR HEART

PSALM 37:4

When I was a twelve-year-old boy, every evening just before supper would find me in our back yard looking skyward. I was watching for the airline that traced a path toward the setting sun on its way from Chicago to Des Moines, Iowa. The rumble of its two powerful engines was like music to my ears. This was the era when the Douglas DC-3 was the premier aircraft being used by the airlines. My dream was to learn to fly and one day be sitting in that DC-3 cockpit as an airline captain. So I relished those evening encounters to dream a little. At that stage of my life I was not focused on what God had planned for my life. Do boyhood dreams come true? Let me tell you about it.

Our MFI (Missionary Flights International) air support ministry was growing and the two eight-passenger Beech 18s we were flying had become too small for the needs of the missions MFI were serving. The next step up to a larger aircraft would be the proven commercial and military workhorse, the Douglas DC-3/C-47. So I began collecting data on just how this thirty-passenger airplane would increase MFI's capability for missions. It was during this time that a Christian businessman from Indiana contacted me to see if MFI could

CAPT. DON H. BELDIN

airlift a work team of fifteen men to help missions in building churches, medical clinics, and mission houses. I could see a new area of need opening up, so I began looking for the Lord's leading to the right airplane to meet this need.

I had a call from a pilot friend saying that Moody Bible Institute had been given a corporate DC-3 and it was for sale. I got on the telephone and found that it was true since Moody Aviation did not have a use for a large twin engine airplane in their missionary pilot training program. I was scheduled to be in a mission conference in Atlanta in two weeks, so I made plans to drive up to Moody Airport in East Tennessee. Looking back, I can see how the Lord was answering prayer and preparing MFI for a larger ministry to missions.

The airplane was beautiful as it sat there on the Moody Aviation ramp. The rest of the day was spent looking the airplane over and going over its records. It had been owned and flown for the past twenty years in executive service by a large corporation in Bridgeport, Connecticut. The aircraft was in excellent condition, and other than changing the cabin from executive configuration to passenger seating, it was ready to enter the ministry!

Moody offered the airplane to MFI for $35,000 knowing it would be used in mission service. But that was $35,000 more than we had—I believed God would provide the funds although I didn't know how He would do it. Undeniably, my faith was small, for I asked for a ninety-day option to purchase the DC-3 which they granted. When I got back to my office, I got on the phone calling some key supporting churches and pastors who I had flown to visit near-mission fields in the West Indies. The Lord opened doors, and within a week I had a month-long fundraising itinerary. God wonderfully blessed us as I visited these churches and told them how this airplane would help missions and the missionary families we served. The key was that these were mission-minded churches with missionaries they supported being helped by MFI's air support ministry. I made no apology for asking them to give substantially to underwrite this step forward. What I had thought might take as much as ninety days to raise that $35,000, God provided in just thirty days! Praise the Lord!

Soon I was on an airline winging my way back to Tennessee to purchase and fly home our first Douglas DC-3 aircraft. What an exciting time it was for me! Certainly God had taught me a lesson about exercising personal faith encouraged by *"Call unto me and I will show thee great and mighty things which thou knowest not"* (Jeremiah 33:3, KJV). God was preparing me for the bigger challenges that lay ahead in His development of Missionary Flights International. We had come from a fledging air support ministry for a few missions to a list of over 175 Bible-centered missions and over 600 missionary families.

I was not yet type-rated in the DC-3, which is required if you are going to fly as PIC (pilot-in-command) of any aircraft over 12,500 pounds. The missionary pilot friend who tipped us off to the Moody airplane and was type-rated in the DC-3 agreed to occupy the right seat as my instructor pilot. On a frosty morning in January, we departed Elizabethton, Tennessee, on course to Palm Beach International Airport. We were just crossing the George/Florida line with Jacksonville on the nose when it hit me! Here I was seated in the captain's left seat in the cockpit of a DC-3—the very airplane that as a boy I had regularly watched fly over our town in Illinois. And I remembered my boyhood dream! I actually was living it! PTL! And the scripture verse of Psalm 37:4 KJV flooded my mind and soul: *"Delight thyself also in the Lord, and he shall give thee the desires of thine heart."* Wow! Yes! This had been my dream, and how faithful are His promises when we also have followed verse five— *"Commit thy way unto the Lord; trust also in him, and he shall bring it to pass."* Wow! It brought goose bumps up and down both arms. I could hardly keep from shouting over the roar of those two big radial engines just outside the cockpit windows. I had met the conditions, and He had kept His word. What a wonderful God we serve! And what a gift of remembrance the Lord had given me on this my very first DC-3 flight!

THE REST OF THE STORY

We were in trouble, maybe BIG *trouble!* The loose sheet metal battery cover on the top of the right wing center section had made the control yoke in my hands shake. Slowing the airplane down had caused the nose to start to pitch over—I was losing control of the aircraft! Power and airspeed were back up to 145 mph, and my elevator control was restored.

We were now in a shallow decent and within twenty minutes of our landing at PBIA. My mind was racing through what was ahead and how I should plan the approach and landing with an unstable aircraft. I knew I would not be able to slow the airplane down to the normal final approach speed because I would lose the elevator control below 145. The normal approach speed for the Twin Beach was 100 mph. It was almost unthinkable to land the airplane at that speed! This was an airplane that was notorious for leaving a runway in what is called a "ground loop" if the pilot didn't stay with it. Among pilots, the Beech 18 was sometimes referred to as the "Twin Beast" because it was a tail dragger—meaning it was a tail wheel airplane. A botched landing could be disastrous! Thank God I would be landing on 9L, which was 7,790 feet long. I would need every foot of it to get this bird stopped.

Approach control turned me over to the PBIA control tower, and I was given 9L for landing. I had reported our emergency to approach control who passed it on to the tower controllers. My plan was to make about a three-mile final to buy some time to get the power adjusted to keep the airspeed up, establish a shallow decent, and ratchet up my preparedness for the landing. Normally on final to a landing, you lower the aircraft flaps, but I reasoned lowering any degree of flaps might aggravate the elevator control factor. I didn't want to take that chance at that low altitude. Then I wondered what lowering the landing gear might do to the stability of the aircraft. But I hit the gear down switch, ready to retract it if the airplane even hinted that the nose was pitching down. The gear came down, and I still had elevator control. I felt confident now that I had the experience and skill to handle the aircraft at this much higher than normal touchdown speed, but I sure needed the help of my unseen copilot. I breathed a quick prayer as the runway threshold was coming up fast. The control yoke continued to shake. Now it was show time!

As we blew past the threshold, I learned later that an instructor friend of mine was sitting with a student in a Cessna 150 at the end of the runway waiting for takeoff clearance. He saw the Twin Beach approaching, recognized it was one of the MFI aircraft, then couldn't believe the speed that I was carrying for a *landing!* He was so puzzled by why that he taxied back to the ramp to wait for me to return from clearing customs/immigration.

Was I up to the challenge of this landing? Well, if there was ever a time to "grease" it on, it was now. And as it turned out, I did manage a grease job landing! Touch down was 145 mph, and I carefully lowered (landed) the tail from the wheel landing that we made, then gradually applied the brakes. We took the full length of that nearly 8,000 foot runway and turned off on the taxiway at the very end. Another prayer was in order—*"Thank you Lord!"* As we taxied into the customs/ immigration ramp, I think my passengers were uttering their own prayer of thanks too.

What caused the shaking of the control yoke and the pitching over as I attempted to lower the airspeed? The next day I called the Beechcraft Factory and ran the whole scenario past their chief engineer. He said that undoubtedly that flapping loose battery cover disturbed the slipstream flow of air over the wing which was in line with about one third of the horizontal stabilizer and elevator. The disturbed flow over the elevator caused it to oscillate, transferring it to the control yoke. The pitching over as the airspeed was bleeding off was because it had changed the stall airspeed at which the elevator was effective. We had only about two thirds of the elevator control surface controlling the airplane.

It had been a very tense half hour of flying, and I don't think I will ever forget it. Later I thought, *What if a less experienced new Beech pilot had been flying that day? What would he have done? Would he feel he HAD to land at the normal airspeed?* Whatever skill that was evident that day was because God gave it at a time that it was sorely needed. But my guardian angel was sorely overworked!

THAT FINAL FLIGHT

It comes to every pilot—the day when you make your last takeoff and landing! You may not know it beforehand, but that day will come! That final day came to me when I walked up the aisle of the Douglas DC-3 and entered the cockpit for the last time—sat down in the left seat for the last time—went through the pre-start and starting check list for the last time—heard those two big Pratt & Whitney radial engines roar to life for the last time—and taxied to the runway for the last time. I was unaware that this would be my last flight!

In the preceding chapters, I have recounted the experiences that God has allowed me to come through. In each one, it was evident to me that He brought me through as my unseen Co-pilot. I have enjoyed reliving those experiences with you—it is as vivid today as though it were only yesterday. Remember the song, "*Those were the days, my friend, we thought they'd never end . . .*" but they will!

So it is with each of us—you may not be a pilot, but there will come a day when we will do the routines of life for the last time. The question is what would you do if you knew that this was your last day? You'd probably live that day differently than all the others. But, most of us won't know when we have hugged a loved one for the last time, played golf for the last time, gone shopping for the last time, and done a multitude of everyday things for the last time. That's why we need

CAPT. DON H. BELDIN

to be prepared for that last day, just like a pilot has prepared for a flight to his destination!

Whether you are a pilot or not, life has a takeoff and a destination landing. The takeoff is the moment we take a last breath, and the landing destination is in eternity. If we have prepared for this "flight" it will be a perfect landing in heaven. The preparation key is having taken *Jesus Christ as your personal Savior!* That preparation must precede the day of our "takeoff."

May I leave you, dear reader, with a last thought to consider. I quote from God's Word, the Bible: *"For God SO loved the world, that he gave his only begotten Son, that whosoever believeth in him should not perish, but have everlasting life"* (John 3:16, KJV). Make it personal by replacing "the world" with your name. Then, and only then, will you be ready for that "final flight" to your eternal destination. I'm ready, are you?

When Christ returns, as the Bible assures us He will, then if you have prepared, I will meet you there. Until then, I remain, *"Yours for a meeting in the air."*

Photo Gallery

Beechcraft Model 18 - Chp. 1 - Big Trouble
at 8,000 Feet

Piper Cub - Chp. 3 - Those Exciting First Lessons

40 HP Taylorcraft - Chp. 4 - Hayfield Flying

Piper Cub - Chp. 5 - First Solo

Three Taylorcraft 40 HP - Chp. 7 - Reliving Those Barn
Storming Days

Stearman PT-17 - Chp. 8 - How Much Was That Airplane?

Stearman - Chp. 9 - The Thrill of Open Cockpit Flying

Vultee BT-13, WWII Basic Trainer - Chp. 11 - Twenty Exciting
Minutes in a BT-13!

Waco **UPF, WWII** Primary Trainer - Chp. 12 - Who Turned
Out the Lights?

Bamboo Bomber **T-50** - Chp. 16 - Flying the Bamboo Bomber

Cockpit of the Cessna T-50

Douglas DC-3 - Chp. 22 - The Desires of Your Heart